ged 16)

The Author

Pamela McKeown was educated at Clifton High School, Bristol, and at the Froebel Educational Institute. She has taught pupils of all ages in independent, experimental and maintained schools, has trained general and specialist teachers, both non- and post-graduates, and has lectured to every sort of lay and professional audience.

Previously Head of the Education Department in Eastbourne College of Education, Mrs McKeown is now Inspector of Nursery and Infant Education and Playgroups Adviser to the City and Council of Bristol. She spent October 1972 working as Educational Consultant to Vancouver School Board, and was subsequently guest lecturer at the University of Illinois.

Reading
A basic guide for parents
and teachers

Reading
A basic guide for parents and teachers

Pamela McKeown
*Inspector of Nursery and Infant Education,
Bristol L.E.A.*

Routledge & Kegan Paul
London and Boston

First published in 1974
by Routledge & Kegan Paul Ltd
Broadway House, 68–74 Carter Lane,
London EC4V 5EL and
9 Park Street,
Boston, Mass. 02108, U.S.A.
Printed in Great Britain by
Richard Clay (The Chaucer Press) Ltd
Bungay, Suffolk

ISBN 0 7100 7418 2 (C)
      0 7100 7424 7 (P)
Library of Congress Catalog Card No. 73–85428

To David and Katharine,
without whom this book
would never have been written

Contents

Introduction

Why yet ANOTHER book on reading?

There is much uncertainty and anxiety among parents and teachers as to how their children can be motivated to read and write, and taught these techniques rapidly and permanently.

This book is an attempt to offer, in non-technical language, a simple account of modern educational practices which can be adapted to local methods and individual approaches, used with any reading scheme or none and which parents can read with a view to helping their children without interfering with their school.

We are educating children today for an unknown and unpredictable future. They will need to develop resources to cope confidently with a constantly changing environment. They will need to be flexible and adaptable in their powers of thought, to be able to project their own ideas and assimilate those of others with accuracy and the minimum of misunderstanding. They will need to be able to use divergent or convergent thought at will. They will need to be able to judge by objective and subjective methods; to think creatively and to use language with precision.

Although first-hand experience is the most telling, it can also be too slow, and man, to survive, must be able to use other men's ideas and discoveries—the products of their investigations and research— 'to stand on the shoulders' of those who came before them or who are their contemporaries.

The above depends on powers of speech, techniques of listening and command of reading skills. The connection between the development of intelligence and the development of language is known to be very close, but, exactly how, when and where to begin to foster their development is often doubtful.

The approach described in the following chapters is an environmental one, based on the natural learning impulses of play and what is known about the normal sequences of child development. Our environment is both human and physical: the people we come into contact with and the animate and inanimate aspects of our surroundings. When babies are immobile the environment must be brought to them, but as mobility develops children move out into their environment, explore it and seek to master it. This interplay with the

I

environment is education in the most all-embracing sense of the word. Through this interplay human beings move successfully towards maturity or, unfortunately, remain immature and unsuccessfully adapted to the demands of adulthood.

Professor Carstairs defined a mature person as:

One who shows a realistic grasp of his environment
A sense of conviction about his identity
An ability to cope with practical tasks
An ability to establish deep personal relationships.

It is well-nigh impossible to develop the ability to do any or all of these things without language in which to think and with which to discuss.

Since more has become known of the vital importance of the pre-school years—the under-five-year-olds—so parents and educationists alike seek to ensure the provision of nursery education for all who wish for it. Circular 8/60, which prohibited increased nursery provision by the state, was withdrawn in December 1972 in the White Paper *Education: a Framework for Expansion*, but meanwhile many parents substituted 'Do It Yourself' in the shape of playgroups. The best of these have done much to offer learning situations for the pre-school years and many more playgroup leaders and parents are now aware of the need to foster language development.

It is hoped that this unpretentious book may be of interest to parents (particularly playgroup leaders), teachers and students in training to work with children as future teachers, nursery nurses or hospital staff, and that both they and the children they serve may enjoy their growing-up process that little bit more. The help that the writer has received from her own son and daughter, those children she has taught, her past college students and her present teacher colleagues is incalculable but is gladly acknowledged. The mistakes are entirely her own work.

Opinions expressed in this book are those of the author and do not necessarily reflect the views or policy of Bristol L.E.A.

1 Language development

Collingwood: 'Every piece of language is an offshoot from an original language of total bodily gesture.'

In July 1970 the Department of Education and Science issued *Reports on Education* no. 64, in which was stated:

Research and experience are bringing greater understanding of how children learn and the difficulties they encounter. The teacher's task is to make the best possible assessment of children's needs and to use professional skills to meet those needs. This involves creative thinking and imaginative work; it also demands a careful selection of books and materials from among the profusion of commercially produced reading schemes which purport to help children to learn to read but sometimes impose language upon them. Even a systematic approach will only succeed if motivation to read is considered at every stage.

Time was when such commercial books and materials were only advertised in professional journals which teachers can be presumed to read. Nowadays some publishers seem to be cashing in on the anxiety of parents to speed up the process of learning to read and some advertisements seem designed to increase this anxiety. There is even an American book which exhorts parents to start teaching reading to their babies! It is the writer's view first, that parents can do a very great deal to help their children *want* to learn to read, but that, unless they have studied the techniques of *teaching* reading—in the way that student teachers do, for three years, in a good college of education—they can do most good by being imaginative parents, and by leaving the teachers to do the job (which indirectly they are paid for by *all* parents) for which they trained. Why keep a dog and bark yourself?

Second, trained and experienced teachers are daily under pressure to examine and select from the enormous volume of books and materials on the market and are frequently bewildered as to what to choose, and even whether a new idea is a worthwhile vehicle or a bandwagon! The only thing we can really *all* be sure about is that the development of language is essential if we are to read and write

3

effectively. Language only develops if we want it to; and who was the cynic who wrote: 'If we taught children to speak they'd never learn'? It really all depends on what you mean by teaching. The good mother teaches her child to speak, and *want* to speak, from the day he is born.

What is the difference between speech and language? The dictionary draws this distinction:

Language—the expression of ideas by words or articulate sounds. Any manner of expression.

Speech—faculty of uttering articulate sounds in words. Language which is spoken.

It is worth spending a moment or two on considering proverbial sayings such as:

'Sticks and stones may break your bones but words can never hurt you.'
'Actions speak louder than words.'
'Why don't you say what you mean?'
'Words fail me.'
'It was too lovely for words.'

While poets take us further with:

Kahlil Gibran, *The Prophet*, 'And even stumbling speech may strengthen a weak tongue.'
Abraham Cowley wrote in *The Prophet*: 'Words that weep and tears that speak.'
Thomas Gray, *Progress of Poesy*, 'Thoughts that breathe and words that burn.'
Charles Reade: 'The human craft of writing, which, though commoner far, is so miserably behind the godlike art of speech.'
Publius Syrus, 'Speech is a mirror of the soul: as man speaks, so is he.'
Lewis Carroll wrote 'Jabberwocky', and other writers have contributed new words to our vocabulary by inventing nonsense words, which we use because they are more expressive than traditional ones; and how is it that the rearrangement of neutral letters—even the phrase 'four-letter' word—can result in such emotional disturbance? 'Love', 'work', 'life' and 'word' are all four-letter words, yet we all know that these are not the ones in mind.

One of the most telling differences between man and other animals is his power of speech. Animals *communicate* but man's *words* are more effective than their *sounds*, being capable of finer interpretation. Words can communicate facts and ideas, and, when recorded, cross barriers of time and space. Some human sounds are more subtle at times than words; equally words gain or lose force according to the way in which they are spoken. The very fact that I am compelled to use italics demonstrates the loss of emphasis in the written as opposed to the spoken word, and hence the loss in meaning. Words can arouse physical and emotional desires; cause bodily changes—for example most people's mouths water at the mention of lemon or frying bacon; lead to actions that change the course of history—'Who will rid me of this turbulent priest?'; have legally binding significance in the form of vows or oaths; or be of totally ephemeral importance. Words can make or break tension, cheer or depress, antagonise or comfort, be said seriously or in jest, but none of this can happen until they are *understood*. Misunderstandings can have serious or comic results—and words can be used with intent or without knowledge of the consequence. All this adds up to the fact that words can be the instrument of communication; but equally that words can be a barrier to the transmission of thought.

Words are frequently used in an attempt to transfer knowledge or information, spoken or written. First-hand experience is often considered to be the best way of learning anything. So indeed it is; and at first, and in the early part of human life, the only possible way. But this is too slow a method for the short span of human life and the demands made on a human being. It is too slow. We need other people's ideas and discoveries—every sort of investigation that has been recorded.

Words—the essential tools of thinking

Dr Susan Isaacs wrote:

> Words are the essential tools of thinking, and without them the child's understanding will inevitably be handicapped. Think of the passion of the ordinary child for naming things, and his delight in new words and phrases! Much is going to be lost to the child who has not this fine instrument of knowledge and communication—much of understanding and of social experience.

Note that Dr Isaacs says that without words the child's understanding will inevitably be handicapped. Many people would consider the reverse to be true, that without understanding a child will not learn to speak. This might appear a paradox—and both statements are, in fact, true. This book is not the place for an academic study of language, speech or the development of intelligence (there are plenty of books available in these areas for those readers who wish to consult them) but there is no shadow of doubt nowadays that the development of intelligence is inextricably interdependent and interwoven with the development of language, and that speech is a vital part of language development (concept formation is referred to in more detail in chapters 3 and 4). Equally the development of language and the development of an emotional balance are closely bound up.

Words—the release of emotion

Every parent and teacher has personal experience of the emotional release of language used by children in anger—and how the need to express aggression in physical terms is reduced when insults and angry words can be offered instead. There are few adults who never resort to swearing—and even inanimate objects can be the provocation, though living creatures, animal and human, are similarly stimulating (provoking?). Some people feel less in the wrong if they swear in a foreign language. We need to recognise that a swear-word would lose its value as an emotional release if we did not intend it to be shocking and out of context. 'Bloody' when applied to a cut hand has a totally different significance when used as an expression of annoyance—and some users are quite unaware that it is a corruption of 'By our Lady', which was once a religious oath and therefore distasteful on religious grounds to those who *do* know.

Summary   Language is intensely personal—closely interwoven with the development of intelligence—and is both the cause of and the result of emotions in the originator and receiver.

Language

Language is also given extra point and significance in the context of the culture pattern in which it is used; and whether it is associated with religious or civil ceremony.

Language has special significance in ritual. Many civilisations have believed that the use of someone's name gives the speaker power over the person. As a result some names were too holy even to be spoken, or written, in full. Spells and incantations almost invariably include the name of the person who is to be influenced, blessed or cursed. Fairy tales include such magic sayings as 'Open

Sesame!' (in fact the name of a food grain!), 'Abracadabra', or nearer our own day, 'supercalifragilisticexpialidocious'. Parents and teachers alike know very well the power of names as applied to children—to be able to name a child is a great steadier of his behaviour! We all like to be remembered by name—it gives us importance, status and/or prestige. This is recognised in general social intercourse, in phrases like 'a name to conjure with' (note the reference to magic), 'name-dropping', 'lending your name to a transaction', 'a name which opens doors' or 'a name it will pay to remember'.

We usually adapt our manner of speech and choice of words to the social occasion. There are formal and informal styles of address; technical words which we reserve for occasions when we are in a selected group of people who share a skill or background or a particular craft; we speak differently when we are sure of our position or are seeking acceptance; when we have nothing to gain or everything to gain; we flatter; we seek to diminish; we take infinite trouble to be understood or we may even try to confuse; we use words with intent to encourage, shame, help or hinder—and all this has to be learned.

Summary Speech is not a skill which will develop automatically with the maturity of the nervous system—like walking for example. Children learn to walk (unless they are prevented from moving) as their nervous system develops.

Illingworth: No amount of practice can make a child sit, walk, talk or acquire other skills until his nervous system is ready for it. On the other hand, delay in the acquisition of skills may be caused by depriving the child of the opportunity to practise them when sufficient maturation has occurred.

We call these moments 'sensitive' or 'critical' periods (ref. *Plowden Report*, para. 28).

A good mother teaches her child to speak and want to do so

It is common knowledge that parents wait with some excitement to see if their baby will walk or talk first; and take a real pride in either achievement, whether or not they have actually helped their baby to progress. Earlier, I wrote that a good mother teaches her child to speak and *want* to speak from the day he is born. The wish to speak is, of course, the essential, and this is developed chiefly by being spoken to. Had the parents waited in silence for their baby to talk this would naturally not have encouraged him to do so.

Normal sequence of speech development

A baby reacts to birth with a shriek of protest and if, as sometimes happens, he does *not* cry, the doctor or nurse takes steps to see that he does, for the baby must immediately breathe for himself if he is to live. Before he is born his oxygen supply is provided by his mother through the delicate membranes which separate her bloodstream from her baby's, but, at birth, he starts the long journey from total dependence to independence and begins to learn to make contact with his fellow human beings by sound, gesture and later words. Some authorities claim that the unborn child makes sounds—certainly he reacts to loud noises with a sudden start.

At first a mother may be quite unable to recognise the cry of her own baby and to distinguish it from those of other babies. Sooner or later, not only can she single out the cry of her baby but she can eventually recognise the feelings (emotions) which prompted the crying. This is by no means always misery. Paediatricians tell us that babies cry for exercise and gain satisfaction by so doing. Obviously no response is then required by the mother. Other cries are very different and may be appeals for help. In ascending order of importance, they are probably pain or discomfort, caused by hunger, apprehension, fear (particularly of noise or falling) or dirty nappies. This is a shrill, piercing cry and we feel an urge to respond. Rage or disappointment is different and is usually unaccompanied by tears. A more musical and rhythmical cry—but poignant—expresses grief and is always accompanied by tears and demands comfort. The most harrowing of all is luckily seldom heard—the cry of the baby in despair, accompanied by the breakdown of personality and the end of the will to live.

Babies appear to experiment with different tones of crying, especially while awaiting sleep. Later as a baby gains more control over his speech organs he plays with his voice too—discovering that he can coo and gurgle, moan and whimper—and that his lips and tongue allow him to make explosive sounds. Repetition results in spontaneous sounds becoming intentional and he learns to imitate the sounds he hears. Some babies learn to mew like cats for example. Most important of all he learns the social value of certain sounds and begins to understand cause and effect in his efforts. Certain sounds bring his mother to him, make her smile or frown, even result in company and being played with! Soon he communicates—that is, makes sounds with consciously desired results—or responds to his mother. (N.B. The use of a dummy may well prevent a baby from vocalising and may thus retard speech development.)

If the mother is imaginative she will talk to the baby whenever she is near and he is awake, as well as when she handles him in her daily care. There are many studies of babies which prove beyond doubt that the one-to-one relationship of a mother and baby (or mother substitute) is essential if satisfactory emotional and language development is to take place. Babies in institutions are less vocal, even before they are eight weeks old. Tests have shown a correlation between the development of intelligence in the three-year-old and the mother's concern with language during this period.

Gwen Chesters: 'A little baby feels and then he behaves: he feels angry and he cries with rage. An older child feels and then thinks before he behaves.'

The earliest perceptions of the baby

Food, warmth, comfort, or lack of it, are intensely emotional in reaction and as well as responding physically the child immediately responds in sound. As anyone knows who has taken a baby out of his bath, he becomes angry all over—very often rigid with fury and scarlet from head to foot and there is no difficulty in interpreting his cries as anger. Equally the change to relaxation and pleasure of a feed when he is hungry may again be accompanied by sounds as well as gestures. Loving physical contact and successful feeding experiences are a major contribution to the effective development of speech.

As with feeding, so with excretion. It has been known for centuries that a baby urinates on those he loves; similarly his stool is his first gift—speedily withheld as a token of disapproval. If wisely and sensitively handled by his mother, excretion experiences lead to a generous, warm and loving relationship with her and later with his family. Too early or severe toilet training can have long-lasting deleterious results. A mother early recognises the sounds made by a baby ready to excrete and if she responds can foster the beginning of co-operation and social awareness. It is well worth the time and effort involved.

It is customary now to inspect new-born babies very thoroughly. It is obvious that a baby must possess adequate physical speech apparatus, i.e. sufficient hearing to discriminate sounds and certain mouth and throat structure. If he also develops normal sight, he is stimulated by the facial expressions of his mother—and later of his family—into repeating sounds which cause him to receive attention and approval. He quickly builds up a passive vocabulary, i.e. an understanding of various words. Later he becomes able to imitate these and slowly to build an active vocabulary, that is, words which he can use to convey meaning. Domestic animals share the power to acquire a limited passive vocabulary, but this can easily be shown to depend more on timbre than words. Similarly babies respond for a long time to the tone of voice rather than to the words used.

Most babies start by using individual words, mainly nouns; and naturally, those of most significance in his life. The emotional response to sounds like Da-da-da and Ma-ma-ma lead to these being well worth making again. It is, therefore, obvious that the more the baby is talked to and listened to the quicker he will understand and value words. As the baby learns to crawl and later to walk, his experiences widen enormously, but until he is mobile the environment has to be brought to him. Again, the imaginative mother will do this—not festooning his pram with dangling toys and rattles—but selecting one or two worthwhile textures and shapes, so that his spontaneous exploration of his body is widened into his exploration of his environment. The baby who is confined to his cot and his pram for long periods and also deprived of companionship, is unlikely to develop into the interested alert language learner. When he can sit up he should be firmly supported by pillows and placed where he can see life and be seen by people who will respond to him and wait for him to respond to them.

During their second year many babies are beginning to string words together. This period has been described as telegraphic speech. Once again the baby is dependent on his mother to fill the gaps and to present full sentences, so that his need to communicate is balanced by his growing ability to do so, and the confusion of his environment gradually becomes sorted out and meaningful. Throughout this time the imaginative mother has shared other experiences with him: he will have been cuddled and rocked, sung to, shown things—pictures in books—his body handled lovingly, with excitements like 'This little pig'. We can hope that his father has enjoyed him too and that the baby has had the richness of another smell, and feel and voice—and perhaps more exciting movements or viewpoints, like seeing the world from his father's shoulders, crawling between his legs, getting his hair tangled in his father's buttons, listening to his watch and so on. All such experiences give meaning to sounds and ultimately to words, and no school can do this for the very young child. The effects of deprivation start very early—and some appear to be irreversible. It looks as though the art of speech is tied closely to the earliest developmental stages of children, and that the flowering period of language comes for most children between their third and fifth birthdays. Compensatory programmes for disadvantaged children have had disappointing results, and there is no doubt that the richest background for children is that of a home where they are loved and talked to, listened to and played with, so that they have something to say and someone to say it to.

It is also vitally important that the home should have books, and adults who read as a matter of course. Much of children's development results from their imitation of older siblings and the adults with whom they live. Although there has been an increase in sentence length and vocabulary size of schoolchildren during the last twenty to thirty years, according to the Department of Education and Science there are still very large numbers of houses with less than five books in them (29 per cent). It is, of course, very easy to borrow books from public libraries, so this could be remedied if parents understood the necessity, but a borrowed book is not the same as one of your own, to read and re-read whenever you wish.

Summary Children learn to speak by being spoken to and listened to. Parents can, therefore, make a major contribution to the ease with which children will learn to want to read if they enjoy their baby's company and appreciate his efforts to communicate with them. Until he can move into the environment, it must be brought to him.

Structure of language

Language has both meaning and structure. Words have to be identified and later strung together in an accepted order if meaning is to be transferred from one person to another. It is always very difficult to remember that the meaning a word has for the speaker may not have the same meaning in the hearer's vocabulary. No one is yet certain how we learn this ordering of words, or how children transfer their understanding of syntax. It is only when their attempts are unsuccessful that we notice, and even then do not usually comprehend the magnitude of their task. For example, 'I'd better do that bettn't I?' is wrong, but 'I should do that shouldn't I?' is right! How do we know?

By the age of six or seven years most children have acquired control of a very complicated organisation of words. They may well feel like Molière who once remarked, 'For forty years I've been talking prose without knowing it.' They will possess a passive and an active vocabulary, be able to use long sentences, varied parts of speech, more sophisticated grammar or a degree of colloquial and formal speech. Many children of this age can play on words, make jokes, devise riddles or use a double meaning. They are normally speaking rhythmically, using inflection to convey meaning and intention, and have decreased their earlier tendencies to repeat the adult's own utterances. They no longer talk whether anyone is listening or not, but require a hearer; they learn to consider the speaker's point of view, to try to influence, to insist on their own viewpoint or even to abandon it in favour of another's—a far cry from egocentricity (unawareness of others) and a long step towards socialisation.

We still do not know how this is achieved—we only know it is *not* achieved without the constant support and affectionate interest first of his mother and father, later of his family, and later still, of other human beings. It is not achieved unless he has been loved and has learned to love in return. We also know that if children have not developed a good command of language before they start compulsory schooling around the age of five, it is appallingly difficult, if not impossible, to remedy the situation.

Summary A good speech model and emotional support are essentials in learning to speak, and the critical period for developing this skill is pre-school.

Rousseau said, 'What is the good of teaching children to read if they hate books?'

Changes in society and our culture pattern have resulted in a paradox. It is both less and more necessary to be able to read. Less necessary because so much entertainment nowadays is offered by television, radio, cinema, theatre—or perhaps bingo halls. The telephone is widely used where the letter once was; people are more mobile and able to travel, when once books were a major source of private and family entertainment and conversation and letter writing were held in high esteem. Conversely we are far more documented: forms have to be read and filled in, there are more signs and advertisements to be read, there is a vast increase in newspapers, magazines and other pulp literature. Records for pleasure and business purposes must be kept and cannot all be put on microfilm, tape or computers' memories. The plight of the non-reader or the poor reader is still acute. So much of one's chances in school, and even more in higher or further education, are dependent on the ability to read with ease, speed and some would say with pleasure. Small wonder that parents and teachers alike consider reading of such great importance. Not a subject itself, it is the means of access to nearly all of them.

It is a sad reflection on our educational system that many children leave school with so tenuous a grasp of the skill of reading that it is rapidly lost. In the writer's view there is minimal value in teaching children to read if it is accompanied by fear or distaste. Anything so learned is speedily unlearned. The purpose of the following chapters is to suggest ways in which children can learn to read so that their enjoyment of words is heightened and their grasp of the skill permanent and with no overtones of dislike or expectation of failure. The writer believes that many methods 'work' and that the teacher's skill lies in her knowledge of alternative methods and her ability to teach each child in the way best suited to his individual gifts and problems.

Importance of parental support

Parents help or hinder according to how well they support the teacher, whether they ask to have the method by which their child is learning explained, so that they can avoid hurtful or damaging observations and comparisons. Their biggest contribution will be in the provision they can make in their family circle—so that conversation is encouraged, books shared and enjoyed, stories told and invented, rhymes and songs taken as a matter of course—and a quiet confidence engendered that in due course their child will read—and no anxiety displayed that speed is important.

Every sort of expedition is of value *if* it is enjoyed and discussed—from the walk down the road to buy a newspaper or watch the man mending a telephone wire, to the special treat of a day out to celebrate a family festival. For the country child there are all the delights of collecting flowers, leaves, pebbles or wool from the hedgerows but the town child can be well served by the parent who helps him to 'collect' colours in shop windows or on cars, or sweet wrappers or shapes on houses. The essential is the delight in each other's company—the shared experience and the talk that goes with it. This is what makes the 'rich' home. The four-year-old child who said that sore tonsils made a bruise in his throat and his voice 'dark' was not accurate in his choice of words, but no hearer could fail to share his experience and understand what he meant.

Don Fraser quipped, 'The big trouble with communication today is the short supply of those willing to be communicated with.' We may smile, some of us wryly, but the basic truth demands our attention: communication depends entirely on the willingness of the receiver, but willingness alone is not enough, and I shall devote a chapter each to the development of auditory and visual discrimination because these are the major means of verbal communication.

Summary Parents can do much to help their children to develop language, and the emotional significance of language demands much sensitivity and conscious effort on the part of all who work with and care for children.

2 Reading readiness

> Montessori: 'The adult works to perfect his environment, whereas the child works to perfect himself.'
> 'The sooner the worse!'

If we are to define reading 'readiness', we must first define the skill of reading. *The Shorter Oxford Dictionary* gives nine definitions of the noun: the act of reading; time spent in reading; study of books; a lecture; a public recital; the way in which a passage reads; interpretation and rendering; the height of a barometer or thermometer; the formal presentation of a bill to the legislature which is to consider it. The verb merits five definitions: to utter aloud what is written or printed; to discover and understand by signs; to peruse; to study; to learn by observation. In everyday life it is 'to utter aloud what is written or printed' or rather *to be unable* 'to utter aloud what is written or printed' that causes such anxiety to the triumvirate of parent, child and teacher. However, after the early stages most of us spend infinitely more time in silent reading, and here different kinds of skills are needed, for all written material does not demand the same skills when read silently as when read aloud. Some texts require slow, careful, considered reading and re-reading; others need only to be skimmed; other occasions demand the ability to scan for recognition—to select and to reject—while for recreation many of us read at a considerably lower level of vocabulary and style. Reading some foreign languages may require a different eye movement from the left to right, top to bottom of the page which is the normal sequence for English. Such a difference in eye movement is likely to reduce the speed of reading. Some people are unable to read silently (see chapter 5).

What is reading?

The two definitions of reading which seem most useful to my purpose are those of John Downing in his book *tω bεε or not to be*: 'reading consists basically in deciphering a code' and Professor Fred Schonell defines word recognition as 'a combination of the total shape of a word, of groups of letters and of individual letters in it',

15

plus the necessity that 'words must mean ideas, not be merely mechanical patterns' (see chapter 5).

The Americans have a saying 'When all else fails, read the directions!' a sarcastic, yet profound observation. Such a remark assumes that having read the directions we are now equipped to deal with the situation. Unfortunately the ability to read words does not carry with it the ability to understand or interpret them. Any commercial firm can give instances of customers who have read the directions and attempted to carry them out, with disastrous results. Official forms strike dismay in many minds. It is very difficult indeed to communicate through the written and printed word.

The mechanical skill of reading—the 'triple association'

Basically, the mechanical skill of reading consists of:

1 Vision—the ability to recognise and identify words.
2 The ability to speak them accurately or think them accurately.
3 The ability to draw meaning from words spoken or thought.

This 'triple association' is a very complex skill, depending on factors both within and outside our control—but more of that later.

Most of us have very hazy memories of our own difficulties in learning to read, and some people cannot recall a period before they could read. In order to appreciate fully the difficulties encountered by the children you would have to be deprived of:

(*a*) Years of reading experience, both oral and silent.
(*b*) The pleasures you have gained from many types of reading.
(*c*) The greater part of your passive and active vocabulary.
(*d*) Your confidence in your ability to make sense of scripts.
(*e*) Your well-nigh reflex left to right eye movement and many other aspects of your reading skill, such as articulation, diction, inflection and other aspects of expression.

Sensitive or critical periods

As an adherent of educational methods based on developmental philosophy, I believe that there is a psychological moment—the sensitive or critical period—in other words, the best possible moment for learning to read, i.e. the ability to recognise and interpret a symbol such as a word or figure. For most children there is a 'flowering period of speech' which occurs *around* the chronological age of four to five years, when children can acquire a very large spoken vocabulary if they are in a stimulating environment. In a verbally privileged home a child may acquire 5000 words by the age of five, whereas in a verbally deprived home the number may be only 300. This flowering period of speech should be followed by further maturation of the brain which permits the satisfactory acquisition of the skills of reading and writing. Note that historically man must have acquired these skills in the opposite order—writing preceding reading—but that in our civilisation the reverse order is more common.

Lillian de Lissa wrote in *Life in the Nursery School*:

A child's power of learning is not absolute, it is limited by physical structure and neuro-muscular co-ordination. Until the areas in the brain that control physical movement are well-developed it is not possible for the centres connected with thought and mental activity to function well. This is one of Nature's laws which education must respect.

Sensory development

Churchill, *Counting and Measuring*, p. 21:

The suggestion that children should be allowed to move about and play with materials of various kinds is often justified in terms of physical growth needs and emotional satisfactions. What should be understood is that they can learn things about themselves, and about the world around them, through moving about and handling things, that they can learn in no other way, since at these times they are receiving all the vital information that motor sensations alone can yield.

If we accept these two statements—and modern medical research undoubtedly supports them—then schools must offer a richly stimulating environment. As the Department of Education and Science pamphlet, *Learning for a Purpose*, p. 6, puts it: a nursery school 'sets out to provide a world which starts the senses tingling, fires the imagination and opens up vast areas of experience'. This should be equally true of infant and junior schools, surely? Natural and man-made objects and all that is associated with these: sounds, smells, tastes, colours, textures, etc., everything to which we respond, either by acceptance or rejection, and the teacher's responsibility is to help the children to translate this experience into words. The successful teacher verbalises, that is, she puts into words the experience the children are having and, by sympathetic interest and well-phrased questions, coaxes the children into using new words or transferring them from their passive into their active vocabulary (see chapter 4). Obviously, first-hand experience is essential to give meaning to words—hard, soft, hot, cold, wet, dry, come first—and abstractions like kindness or jealousy can only be given point and significance as social contacts widen and are made explicit by an understanding adult.

Aristotle said, 'Nothing is in the mind which was not first in the senses,' and teachers must ensure that children not only have internal and external sensory experiences but that these are linked with language. It is commonly assumed we have five senses—sight, hearing, taste, smell and touch—but in reality the last—touch—has many facets. For example, weight is experienced chiefly internally: the pull on muscles, though it is also experienced as a tactile sensation. We speak of 'butterflies in the stomach', another internal sensation. Tactile sensations are likewise multiple—degrees of heat, texture, pressure, pain and so on, can be distinguished and children helped to select appropriate words with which to describe them. The best foundation for later learning is personal observation and experience—a diversity and multiplicity from which generalisation and abstraction can be developed and stand the test of time.

Reading 'readiness'

Not so long ago it was widely claimed that a mental age of six-plus years was essential before beginning the formal teaching of reading. Personally I know of no accurate way to establish mental age in very young children and, therefore, support the concept of reading *readiness* which combines many aspects of child development. If we consider the following points I believe that we shall have observed children sufficiently well to judge what to offer in the way of suitable experiences and how to stimulate language at the same time.

Summary   May I make it quite clear that I believe we should not simply sit and await reading readiness—as we might wait for the sun to shine or the rain to fall! By means of a prepared environment and the stimulation of good play we can foster and speed up 'readiness'.

Play and its significance

Play is both the motive force and the means of learning. It is a voluntary, enjoyable activity undertaken for its own sake, essential to every child, through which satisfactory development in all aspects of growth should take place. Play should include physical, intellectual, social and emotional types and lead to serenity and stability.

The stages of play

In broad terms, children pass through five stages of play: solitary, spectator, parallel, partnership and group.

1 *Solitary play* may originate in the cradle and be initially concerned with body discovery, slowly widening to exploration of the immediate and later of the total environment. But solitary play should continue through life—perhaps the angler is a typical example?

2 *Spectator play* is an essential part of the socialising process. The nine-month-old baby watching his mother at work or older children at play is beginning to move from total self-awareness—egocentricity —towards integration and identification with others. This type of play again continues through life but can deteriorate into the inability to exert oneself and even into the aggression or hysteria of the sports fans.

3 *Parallel play* is a stage which tends to cause adult anxiety. Children play in the presence of other children without making any attempt to involve the other by gesture or speech. Nevertheless this is a natural stage and yet another movement away from egocentricity.

4 *Partnership play* will be of very short duration at first. Good schools offer equipment to stimulate such play—seesaws and rocking boats which are unsatisfactory for solitary play—home corners, teasets and dressing-up clothes usually result in play when children discover other children are useful play material rather than a threat to their relationship with adults.

5 *Group play* is usually adult-directed at first, and the result of verbal stimulus, and normally disintegrates if the adult moves away. Eventually most children develop enough self-control to support group play—at least for short periods. In its most sophisticated form this develops into adult clubs and societies.

The role of the teacher and types of play

The role of the teacher is a demanding one. She must assess the preschool experience of each child by observing his play proficiency and then seek to complement (complete) the home by the provision of the relevant play material. Satisfactory provision will provide opportunities for growth of self-confidence, for growth in independence; for widening the child's interest in school and his environment; the development of perseverance, concentration and tenacity in problem solving; growth in emotional stability; and increase in powers of speech and comprehension. The children will move forward to more advanced stages of play—social co-operation and self-control. In a satisfying play situation, records will be kept of each child's maturation, and time and interest will be devoted to areas where such progress is not taking place. Imaginative and constructive play is extremely important in the development of language. All children regress from time to time—but consistent regression or abnormal behaviour will need expert help and children should be referred to the school medical service before time is lost.

There are numerous commercially produced record cards for the assessment of reading readiness—but many teachers will prefer to construct their own. In general the following aspects require consideration: physical, intellectual, social and emotional.

1 *Physical*   Is the child generally healthy, alert and energetic? Has he good sight, hearing and diction? Is he well co-ordinated as regards gross muscle development? How good is his fine muscle control—hand/eye co-ordination? Can he handle tools? Can he dress himself easily and speedily? (See chapters 5 and 6 for more detailed consideration of visual and auditory discrimination.)

2 *Intellectual*   Does he show an interest in words and/or books? Can he carry out one or two part orders? Can he listen to a story; follow the thread; recount it? Can he ask questions and understand answers? Can he remember routine; classroom arrangement of materials and storage of tools; recall and describe home events; anticipate birthdays or seasonal festivals? Does he respond to verbal or numerical symbols? N.B. it is often difficult to assess intelligence or the use of it. Children have been considered stupid who were in fact only partially hearing. Do not hesitate to ask for tests by a doctor and/or educational psychologist. It is not a mark of inadequacy as a parent or teacher—quite the reverse.

3 *Social and emotional*   This is probably the most important area of readiness: sufficient emotional stability and maturity to support making mistakes or being disappointed is essential before formal teaching takes place. As children learn so much from each other, they are usually not ready for reading activities until they have a certain amount of successful contact with their peers. Unfortunately this is also the area in which it is often so hard for parents to wait,

without transferring their anxiety to their child which in its turn impedes the growth of emotional stability.

Probably the best guide to reading readiness occurs in imaginative and domestic play. Children can be seen imitating grown-ups reading—or 'reading' to an audience of dolls, even if the book is upside down. My own son used to 'play' the piano only if printed material was on the stand—the *Financial Times* or the telephone directory were equally acceptable. Some children even ask to be taught to read, but this is usually the influence of a verbally privileged home. It is only dangerous when the wish to read is the result of parental pressure and is unaccompanied by delight in stories from books, discussion of pictures, etc. Tactful parent education is then called for—and an appreciation of 'more haste, less speed'. It is an indictment of compulsory schooling and some methods employed that illiteracy exists among young adults. It is evident that the experience of learning to read was so distasteful that as soon as no one compelled them

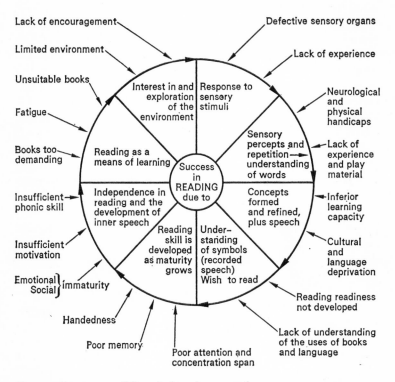

Causes of success or failure in learning to read

to read they ceased to do so, and rapidly lost their skill. J.-J. Rousseau asked more than a hundred years ago: 'What is the use of teaching children to read if they hate books?' What, indeed?

The diagram on p. 21 is an amalgam of points concerned with the acquisition of reading, coupled with reasons for failure.

Paramount in successful teaching of reading are two points:

(*a*) the teacher must organise her approach and have a clear understanding of alternative methods so that she can satisfy individual needs;

(*b*) she must be aware of the vital importance of parental/teacher expectation and the resulting self-regarding sentiment engendered in the child.

As the mother of a dyslexic daughter I am well aware of the debt I owe to teachers who maintained her belief in her ability to learn to read. 'Nothing succeeds like success' and as Charity James wrote, every child needs 'massive experience of success'. The teacher's skill lies in her ability to contrive such success daily, for every child in her class—no small undertaking.

The general public is prone to criticise schools for wasting time in play. It is unfortunate that we have only one word for play in the sense of 'muckin abaht', passing the time, the opposite of work and so on. There are other meanings such as professionals 'playing' matches where 'play' is taken extremely seriously, and no spectator could be unaware of the effort involved. Montaigne (1533–92) wrote, 'Children's plays are not sports, truly they should be noted as their most serious actions' and also, 'He works hard at his play, he plays at doing work', while Melanie Klein warns, 'The inability to play is the mark of the neurotic child' and Dr Winnicott suggests 'for play, like speech, can be said to be given as to hide our thoughts, if it is the deeper thoughts that we mean'.

Summary 'Children Learn What They Live' (Dorothy Law Nolte)

> If a child lives with criticism
> He learns to condemn.
> If a child lives with hostility
> He learns to fight.
> If a child lives with ridicule
> He learns to be shy.
> If a child lives with shame
> He learns to feel guilty.

If a child lives with tolerance
He learns to be patient.
If a child lives with encouragement
He learns confidence.
If a child lives with praise
He learns to appreciate.
If a child lives with fairness
He learns justice.

If a child lives with security
He learns to have faith.
If a child lives with approval
He learns to like himself.
If a child lives with acceptance and friendship
He learns to give love in the world.

Classroom organisation

Many schools have now moved away from the traditional one-teacher-per-class of children selected by chronological age, housed in an isolated classroom. Some schools are fully open-plan. Family or vertical grouping results where the teachers concerned believe that every child is a unique individual and is best served by an environment that stimulates and supports the curiosity which motivates learning. These schools permit free movement so that their pupils work with children both older and younger than themselves—more or less gifted—and with all the adults who work in the school. In an informal working organisation it is believed that language development is stimulated and supported. This sort of organisation is usually described as 'workshop'.

Transitional grouping is favoured by teachers who consider that too wide an age range either puts strain on the youngest or does not demand enough of the oldest, and these group children with eighteen months or two years difference. The philosophy is the same—to help every child to discover and use his ability to move from egocentricity towards socialisation; to stimulate language development and powers of communication in many forms: concrete, spoken and written, representational and symbolic, and to give opportunity for a child to acquire intelligence.

In an informal set-up, organisation, planning and record-keeping are of paramount importance (see chapter 11). Teachers need to consult each other daily or more frequently still in order to ensure that aims and methods which may and should differ from teacher to teacher are nevertheless welded into a consistent and meaningful environment for every child, and progress realistically assessed in order that future teaching and/or experience may be relevant and hence growth be assured, as far as possible. Direct teaching will be given individually, in small and large groups or whole classes, as need dictates. School teaching space will either be purpose-built or adapted to give flexibility for grouping of different sizes. As children mature, longer and longer periods of work on their own become possible and more responsibility for planning the day or week is accepted happily by the children. Total standards of achievement can be expected to rise and positive work attitudes to develop. As the *Handbook of Suggestions for Teachers* (p. 210) puts it: 'The correct timing of educative opportunities is another aspect of the framework of the environment' and (p. 29) 'for to translate experience into words is the basis of intellectual development'.

The teacher's role is to furnish the environment that makes it possible for the pupils to develop reading readiness—and to seize each opportunity as it offers itself to build on this readiness.

3 Symbolism

Comenius (1592–1671): 'The pedagogues, what do they
teach? Words! Words! Words!'

Human communication is obviously not confined to words. There
are many moments when bodily contact is infinitely more satisfying
or reassuring, stimulating or pacifying. Nevertheless, society depends
greatly on human beings who have command over language—and,
even more perhaps, on those who can not only speak more than one
language but who can translate the nuances of one into those of
another. English is possibly the richest language in the world, due in
no small part to recognition that when an exact equivalent does not
exist in English yet another word is lifted from a different language
and quickly interlocked into English. Words like role, nuance itself!,
milieu, verandah, liaison, blitz, aperitif, are fully naturalised. Sometimes we create words, by mistake, such as the childish malapropism
cowardish, hoghedge, or, on purpose, such as fashion's, 'greige', and
furgora; or damn bombage and other wartime slang.

Sometimes jargon goes wild and unfortunate words and phrases
can result, e.g. summatative; normative; weak risky item; self-other
and self-admired differences; judgmental phenomenon.

Nevertheless, some words have double meanings, being used
colloquially to mean one thing and technically to mean quite another,
e.g. model, accommodation, nipple, principal, mouse.

Words are sophisticated symbols

As words are the most sophisticated of all symbols, requiring understanding of the speaker's experience and hence the meaning he
attaches to his words, and a sympathetic effort by the hearer to share
his meaning, we must start by considering other symbols first.

Symbols are as old as man's need to share his feelings, record his
experience or transmit cultural patterns, organisational devices,
religious beliefs, and to master his environment or at any rate not
remain entirely at its mercy. But symbols have to be interpreted as
well as invented. They may have no common element with the object
they represent, yet they may suggest to the mind something pictured

by association with this object and have a strong emotional tie with it. Symbols correctly interpreted increase understanding and meaning. What precedes interpretation of a symbol?

It is common practice nowadays to define certain things as *status symbols*. A new car, a grand house, expensive food and entertainment, ostentatious clothes, sending your child to a school attended by royalty, etc. Some apparently pointless objects are valued—dummy pianos—even by the pair—buying real or fake books by the yard—erecting a TV aerial without possessing a set, have all been known. We have to ask ourselves what *need* is being satisfied? or what do these things *represent* to their owners?

Different types of symbol

A symbol has been defined as:

(*a*) a sign or representation of any moral or spiritual thing by images or properties of natural or material things;

(*b*) the assumption in external things of an inner spiritual meaning;

(*c*) a conventional or arbitrary sign, by means of which the recording of mathematics and science is much simplified, i.e. international shorthand, $£$, $\%$, H_2O, etc.

Goldman wrote, 'A symbol stands for something, it represents it. Every day we use symbols in all kinds of ways. We see them; we act them; we hear them; we speak them.'

Note the order in which he places these, which corresponds to the sequence of human development. Rightly, words come last.

The earliest human symbol with which the baby comes in contact is human touch. Babies respond quickly to cuddling and rocking and are unnerved when held irritably or insecurely. Rapidly this experience is joined by the visual pleasure of watching the adult's face, and this pleasure is speedily reinforced by the social success of being able to respond, i.e. the baby's smile of recognition is rightly treasured by his parents as a sign of growing intelligence, affection and communication. Soon the baby can respond to sound and anticipate the sight of his mother or other familiar person, and his smile may precede seeing her face. The baby's interpretation of this sign or symbol is clear: his own gesture spontaneous.

Signals

As muscular control develops—a smile can be either spontaneous or intentional. We learn as adults to withhold a smile when, although secretly amused, our bringing-up of our children would be jeopardised, we believe, because we know our smile signifies approval to the children. This gesture then has become a *signal*—and will be used either to encourage an action to take place, for instance, smiling at a child to encourage him to dive from a higher board than he is used to, or to reward an action we wish repeated—smiling our thanks for a helpful or courteous action.

Facial expressions are often accompanied by gestures, and sometimes replaced by them. Beckoning and pointing are quickly understood—and babies who cannot speak demonstrate their passive vocabulary by pointing to objects, parts of their body, etc., on command. Spontaneous gesture likewise quickly becomes intentional and also rapidly hardens into symbolic gesture and ritual. The meaning can differ greatly from country to country, and gestures may easily be misinterpreted, with comic or tragic results, leading to the proverbial 'When in Rome do as the Romans do', so that we may not unwittingly cause offence. We have to *learn* to respond to symbols, in fact. Kepes, *Sign, Image, Symbol*, p. 7: 'Only those who have learned to recognise and interpret the meanings of symbols can and do respond to them according to the requirements and expectations of their group' and again, 'over the centuries there has been prolonged and intensive controversy over symbols, especially by those who have refined symbols attributing to them a reality superior to the actual world of our sensory awareness'.

Development of play from symbolic to representational

All parents are familiar with the sequence of children's play leading from symbolic to representational. Quite small children love to offer 'pretend' objects. My own children spent hours running to and fro—later scooting or triking back and forth—fetching imaginary articles from a shop and receiving equally imaginary payment. Their hand movements were sometimes most realistic, conveying a pound of sausages or a bottle of juice—at other times a careless wave of the hand sufficed. Equally they varied in their demands for realism on my part—on one occasion a touch of the palm signified money—on other occasions three pennies had to be implied by three separate movements. Later a stone was offered as the butter and payment demanded in concrete form—a leaf or daisy head. The play was in no way less satisfactory if the child picked the leaf himself and handed it to me to be used as money! Sometimes the 'money' was carefully kept, sometimes immediately discarded, and occasionally, most co-operatively returned so that it would be ready for the next transaction. If one analyses such play it will be obvious that the children see nothing illogical in what appear to us totally conflicting roles and thought sequences.

The symbolism of children's drawings

The symbolism of this play is shortly followed by the symbolism of children's drawings (this subject will be returned to in chapters 5 and 6). Again every parent has received 'letters' consisting of scribbles —the more advanced ones running rhythmically in lines across a page —demonstrating careful observation and imitation of adult writing. The sequence of children's drawings from cephalopods through pancake men to the curious semi-transparent figures is equally well known, and it is not until middle childhood that any anxiety is evinced as to the need for representational drawing of figures—that is, unless some well-meaning adult has interfered and damaged the child's self-confidence and security with his drawings and paintings. Showing 'how' to draw/paint is not only arrogant but can be extremely dangerous in that such advice interferes with the children's thinking and may confuse them to the extent of holding back their intellectual development. At the very least, it is discouraging and may cause the children to regress and repeat whatever drawing *is* approved of instead of venturing further in exploration and experiment. This will naturally hold back progress.

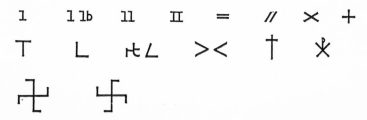

Symbols formed from straight lines. Sarsent or Swastika dates from 4th millennium B.C. Some experts claim it as a sun symbol. Found in Persia, Greece, Cyprus, India, Japan, China, etc.

Interpretation of symbols alters with increased experience or the personality of the interpreter. 'Beauty lies in the eye of the beholder', of course—but there is also the emotional significance which colours our judgment. Few of us are fearless critics in the presence of the creator! Much of the bringing-up process of children involves that they should learn not to speak exactly what they think. Concepts of politeness, honesty and kindness are sacrificed to expediency and good manners—and must be bewildering indeed to young children. It often astonishes me to note the indifference of adults to children's feelings, demonstrated by the criticism offered when viewing their work, and to compare it to the sensitivity with which the same adults react to an implied slight or imagined snub 'read into' an action or word from a friend or colleague. Every teacher needs to guard against the careless comment or hasty assessment which will discourage or hurt a child. I was once vividly made aware of this by a six-year-old. I found him in a corridor pulling the school cat's tail and anguished squawks of the captive smote my heart. Inspired with what I interpreted as moral indignation I said, 'You are unkind to pull the poor cat's tail.' A scarlet face was raised to mine and the owner retorted, 'I aren't pulling. Cat's pulling! I'm holding on!' Happy the child who can protect himself verbally from unfair charges! The situation was sorted out—but I was, of course, in the wrong—incorrectly interpreting a gesture or symbol and attributing the wrong motive.

cephalopod

going upstairs or
climbing a hill

running about
and having fun

angels or
aeroplanes

Children's drawings symbolising (a) human figures, i.e. what is known
(b) movement

Our heritage of story and fantasy

Man's need to understand and master his environment led to the creation of imaginary beings and all the wealth of story and fantasy which is our heritage. Natural phenomena such as thunder and lightning were attributed to supernatural and incredibly powerful gods and goddesses—who nevertheless were subject to human frailties such as jealousy, pride and envy. Truly we create gods in our own image! Man sought to protect himself from ill fortune or disaster by propitiation—gifts of items he himself treasured—or votive ceremonies which frequently included music, dance and incantation. Acceptable behaviour was encouraged and anti-social action discouraged by tales of real heroes of the past—or imaginary human, divine or supernatural beings—and fables, legends, parables, myths, folklore and allegory can all contribute to our understanding of human behaviour and needs. The very fact that many interpretations are possible of the story of the Minotaur, the unicorn, phoenix or dragon, or the character of faun, nymph, siren, elf, dwarf, mermaid, witch or familiars like Pegasus, Sleipnir, St Jerome's lion or even Mary's lamb means that we are forced to question our own motives and behaviour in a wholly desirable way.

Parents and teachers must understand clearly the recurring human need for symbols as a means both of expression and communication if they are to be able to understand the children for whom they are responsible. What are sometimes felt to be moral issues such as true/false, mine/thine or selfish/unselfish can perhaps be more accurately seen as a growth from total lack of understanding of other people and the natural environment and a struggle towards reliable interpretation of events and human contacts. There appear to be many adults who are relatively uncritical of the primitive drawing but who see nothing unreasonable in requiring infinitely more sophisticated techniques and standards in language and behaviour.

Subjective and objective judgments

Before considering the see, act, hear or speak classification of symbols we need to distinguish between subjective and objective reactions. We often believe ourselves to be judging objectively when in fact we are depending on subjective criteria. A quick test is whether the words 'I think . . .' could or should be inserted as a prefix. An objective judgment can be measured by a scale which is universally accepted, e.g. a pound of apples, a metre of string, 10p, are not open to doubt, except so far as the accuracy of balancing, matching or counting is concerned.

Conceptual development

Concepts of beauty—goodness, truth, style, are value judgments, that is, they can or should be preceded by 'I think that . . .' and will alter as the holder becomes better informed or more experienced. As an illustration, we could take the word 'dog'. When my son was eighteen months, he walked beneath a huge dray horse, stroked its tummy and murmured lovingly 'nice goggie'. Certainly he had discriminated some of the characteristics a horse shares with a dog—but his experience was too limited to have classified accurately. Later he and his sister were confused by a Pekinese—expecting it to mew as a cat should! Later still, they could differentiate between most dogs but were brought up short by a Great Dane and Irish Wolfhound as big as calves and a chihuahua as small as a kitten. Learning that relative size did not alter the species 'dog' they moved on to breeds, and for a time 'collected' sorts of dog—slowly but surely differentiating between a standard poodle puppy and a miniature poodle adult. Had their interest continued presumably they could have sharpened their observational powers and increased their experience sufficiently to act as a show judge of some breed of dog, but this would still be a value judgment and subjective—even if accepted by many people.

There has been an attempt lately to reduce the value judgments of the examination process and to try to increase the techniques by which answers can be required which can be marked objectively. The purpose of discussion at this juncture in the book is to suggest to both parents and adults that marks and assessments are themselves symbolic and have to be interpreted and given with caution. It is our growing understanding of the significance to both pupil and parent of marks/grades that has led to a growing unwillingness to use them in school. This I applaud, believing so strongly in the damage to personality and inhibiting influence of comparing one child with another. To put it crudely, there may be motivation to be first rather than third in rank, but I do not believe an equal urge results from the possibility of being 24th rather than 27th—and saddest of all, if anyone is first someone *must* be last. The very act of competitive assessment cuts right across the self-evident facts of individual differences and ignores the knowledge we now possess that children tend to rise or fall to meet the expectations of people with whom they live. Far and away the most influential of these are their parents and teachers—but as they grow up, the value children attach to their peers speedily catches up on this and eventually surpasses it. I believe, therefore, that we must be always on our guard and sensitively aware of the symbolic importance of our facial expressions, our gestures, and all the other signs and signals we offer to the children. Equally we must seek to discover—in the most unobtrusive way—how our actions are interpreted by the children. Here a frank, trusting relationship between home and school is obviously essential if the children's well-being is to be safeguarded.

Recording first-hand experience

We cannot consider symbols without reviewing the many ways in which we attempt to record first-hand experience. One of the earliest ways children display their experience is by re-creating it in play and imitation. We are all familiar with the stage at which a child temporarily becomes another person, object or animal—depending on his home experiences. A sensitive adult is quick to use this facility—helping a tired child to walk home by giving him a stick to ride as a hobby horse—or suggesting we walk like ducks or run like dogs or fly like birds. We get the dinner eaten by addressing him as 'good dog' or the unwilling to bed to be tucked up 'like your teddy bear'.

A little later we join in the pretend shops, schools, processions or other imitative and dramatic play which often involves symbolic rhymes or incantations—and physically play the gesture, counting-out rhymes or stylised movement which convey meaning to the participants. In order to convey knowledge, techniques and skills we may demonstrate, make models or use visual material such as film—all of which is symbolic rather than first-hand experience. We use radio, tape and disc, or flannelgraph and magnet board with its symbolic simplification—which is only helpful (simplified?) if correctly interpreted. Diagrams and maps are still more sophisticated and finally—most remote of all from reality—come words, including those such as 'cleave' which carry diametrically opposed meanings.

Symbols may either break through language barriers, e.g. international codes such as music notation or flags, or be restrictive, e.g. local or national signs which require too much accommodation from the personal and individual viewpoint to be effective, or an excessive amount of knowledge for their interpretation, e.g. scientific or mathematical formulae. Some symbols belong only to national

ceremonies or are religious ritual or the result of the distortion common to advertisement and propaganda. All have to be evaluated and
interpreted.

Emotion and symbolism

Once we are accustomed to communicate by speech we may yet be
thrown back on gesture when the person we address is in vision but
out of earshot. This can be very frustrating, and is possibly the situation young children are frequently in, that is *physically* hearing words
while *mentally* out of earshot as regards understanding them. We
tend to forget the strength of children's feelings and the immediacy
of their need to understand. *We* can often afford to wait because our
experience assures us that a situation is not over threatening or
frightening and that a successful outcome is possible. Pain will pass,
disappointment can be tolerated, misunderstandings can be rectified,
mistakes repaired or losses replaced: children can have no such trust
until experience has taught them. Sometimes an explanation in
words—thought and intended to be comforting—is simply the substitution of one unknown by another. 'A joy shared is a joy doubled.
A trouble shared is a trouble halved.' True enough, but the sharing
is not automatic, and the unknown is normally threatening. We must
not overestimate children's powers of accommodating themselves to
new experiences. Parents and teachers are wise to change only one
part of the environment; ensuring either that new adults be introduced in familiar settings or new surroundings in the company of
known and trusted adults wherever possible.

Visual symbols

Life is so constantly unpredictable that the child who noticed his cat
had eight legs when he ran, four when he walked and none when he
sat down was trusting his eyes. We may smile, but Egyptian tomb
paintings concur. The horse is drawn standing erect, but when it has
eight legs instead of four, this signifies movement! In much the same
idiom, my daughter put two suns in her picture to show it was a very
hot day. Incautious comment or questioning could have destroyed
her ability to think for herself and attempt to pass on her ideas.
Another young child once told me 'First I think and then I draw my
think.' Who am I that I should tell him how to draw and hence how
to think?

As a summary, I shall use Goldman's classification of symbols:

'We see them; we act them; we hear them; we speak them.' The study of painting styles reveals visual symbols in abundance—man's interest in the play of light and attempts to draw in perspective; the impressionists and cubists; the selection and simplification of some modern approaches; the realistic and symbolic use of colour, can all be paralleled in literature. Here again we are brought short by cultural differences—white for joy, innocence and weddings (and if linked with feathers—cowardice, in our country) and for mourning in India: yellow for cowardice and treachery in Europe—for holiness in the East, and so on. People who cannot read words can perhaps read traffic lights; shop signs (not only the medieval barber's pole combined with blood to signify a surgeon; or the brewer's bush, etc.); totem poles or the magic of the Zodiac signs; masks; wool mark and other trademarks; staff and dance notation; flags; heraldry; school, club or university badges and scarves; military and ecclesiastical insignia; barrister's silk or the silk rope to hang the aristocrat; statues and gravestones; maps, meteorological signs. The swastika or sarsent is a fascinating example: one way the symbol of evil and the other—so alike—all is well. Another problem of visual perception allied to handedness—where an error could be catastrophic.

Ritual

Another proverb runs 'Actions speak louder than words!' In normal life we use many actions to signify intention or to control behaviour. We shake hands: kiss for many reasons and in many ways; kneel; bow; salute—we crown with laurels—actually and metaphorically—or we rest on them—metaphorically only—we offer the olive branch and assume an understanding. Some actions are ritualistic: war and victory dances; the maypole; Morris dances and festivity or fertility rites; propitiation dances and those other religious movements, postures or dances; the sign of the cross, or, in order to dishonour religion—the actions and insignia of the Black Mass. Some symbols result from mimicry—natural camouflage of animals leading to devised camouflage of man—imitative behaviour—the show-biz' 'business' or All Fools' Day traditions. Some symbols are an essential part of ceremonies such as baptism, marriage, coronation, penances. Note the close emotional significance attached to all these actions. Modern educational practice has moved away from silence and immobility for young children in the classroom—recognising that movement can itself be communication, and a powerful aid in language development.

Auditory symbols

Probably the most powerful emotive symbol we hear is our own name, closely followed by names for parents, siblings and household possessions. Speech itself derives from emotional sounds—coo, laugh, cry, moan, whimper, sigh and the timbre of voice often carries more meaning than the words used. Contrived sounds signal to us: whistle, hooter, telephone, alarm clock—there are special sounds for approval—we clap, cheer or use words like Hear, hear! Bravo! Encore! Sophisticated arrangements of sounds are made for pleasure or sadness; music, song, poetry, literature or muffled drums, keening and wailing or funeral marches. Some sounds have special significance on certain occasions—church bells, gun salutes, the boatswain's whistle, three knocks for curtain up, morse.

Speech and its development into recorded language

There is subtle difference between words we hear and words we speak, and not only the physical fact that our sinuses and head bones make the sound of our voice different to us and our hearers, nor the fact that a bird can 'talk', using human words without understanding. I imagine no one attributes patriotism to the budgerigar which can say 'God save the Queen'? The symbols we speak are learned first by rote—pure imitation—but later result from the pleasure gained by being listened to and approved of. The resultant repetition leads to precision of speech due to growing powers of aural and oral discrimination, widening experience and social contacts and the need to use this tool.

Most people eventually record words in the form of writing or typing. These symbols are the successors of the pictures, hieroglyphs, characters, letters and figures of earlier civilisations. Fortunately for us, our words are recorded phonically, as opposed to traditional Chinese where thousands of characters must be learned—unfortunately our language is irregular—with numerous alternatives.

Abstract concepts

Out of language—oral and recorded—have developed abstract concepts, resulting in ideas, literature, argument, reasoning, planning, anticipation and other protective and educative devices. Symbols are used to encourage and exhort certain types of feeling and hence behaviour, e.g. the American flag ceremony; national flags and songs; school and other uniforms; passwords and mottoes; trademarks; postmarks, and so on. Buildings are shaped to raise thoughts to heaven or to conceal their function; to promote sales, most packaging and advertisements are full of symbols. Advertising often appeals to our cruder desires—superiority; sexual conquest; intellectual pride; emotions of care or rejection; various sentiments or aspirations or attitudes.

The seer of ancient times has given place to the psychiatrist and his interpretations of the symbolism of dreams. Rorschach tests are used to uncover attitudes and emotional reactions. The nursery rhyme may have significance undreamed of by the mother, e.g. 'Upon Paul's Steeple' where the apples represent the heads from executions, or 'Little Jack Horner', the courtier whose plum was the deeds to a confiscated estate. The visual pun (illustrated in chapter 5) has symbolic significance—but no less misleading is our assumption that our hearers have the same meanings for words as we have!

Parents and teachers must always seek additional ways of making ourselves understood by children and endeavouring to understand them. The choice, timing and style of presentation of symbols to children needs careful thought. What connections have symbols with imagery, imagination and language development? By the very nature of symbols they may often have a double meaning. This is exploited by comedians in their exercise of 'double entendre' but may not be so amusing to the child confused by 'pilot' and 'Pilate' and the flight into Egypt. Pinsent wrote, 'Without words the pupil is prevented from transcending his immediate concrete, perceptual experiences. He cannot proceed to well-developed abstract ideas and general principles, without which science and mathematics as well as ethics are impossible.' I would venture to add that the understanding of symbols is equally necessary. We use visual, auditory and tactile symbols all the time, and eternal vigilance is necessary to ensure that children acquire understanding of these vivid and expressive ways of communication and have a wide choice from which to draw. Teachers can easily rely overmuch on words and we need constantly to remind ourselves that *talking* is not teaching: and *listening* is not learning. That is—it can be—but will take much thought and care and the ability to recognise the occasion when words alone can convey meaning. Communication is both hampered and furthered by symbolism, and the sequence from spontaneous activities to conscious and deliberate attempts to convey information and ideas must not be left to chance. Young children are literal creatures and are puzzled by sayings such as having 'cold feet', 'water in one's veins', being 'chicken-hearted' and so on, and unless unfailingly courteously treated and not laughed at—will be unwilling to seek clarification.

Summary Whitehead:

> The art of free society consists first in the maintenance of the symbolic code; and secondly, in fearlessness of revision, to secure that the code serves those purposes which satisfy an enlightened reason. Those societies which cannot combine reverence for these symbols with freedom of revision, must ultimately decay either from anarchy, or from slow atrophy of a life stifled by useless shadows.

Schools as part of society—and their agents, the teachers, need therefore to review their use of symbols of all kinds.

4 Matching, sorting and grading

Lichtenberg: 'What you have been obliged to discover for
yourself leaves a path in your mind which
you can use again when the need arises.'

In the previous chapter, a rough outline of the development of the
concept of 'dog' was given—referring to this development in the
writer's children. We need now to consider in more detail the
development of concepts and how parents and teachers can help
children to form lasting and accurate concepts. The Nuffield
Mathematics Project took as its motto the Chinese proverb:

I hear and I forget
I see and I remember
I do and I understand

but nothing is mentioned here about the development of language,
without which no check upon the accuracy of seeing or hearing or
worthwhileness of doing is possible. Aristotle wrote, 'Nothing is in
the mind which was not first in the senses'.

Percepts

The response to a sensory stimulus is termed a *percept*. In everyday
use the word perception is frequently applied to an act of vision—
and far less often to the perception of pain, heat and cold, noise, smell
or taste, but each of these sensory responses is a percept. The mental
response to a percept is a rudimentary concept (correct or a misconception) according to whether the percept is accurately interpreted, or, on a subsequent occasion accurately remembered. As the
experience is repeated, and percepts accumulate, so the concept is
built in more detail, and a previous misconception removed or increased in strength.

Concept growth

The process of concept growth is known as *refining or sharpening* the concept, and if experiences are sufficiently varied—and another person present who can help use language—the accuracy should be increased. Without language, concepts can only be blurred and possibly ephemeral. The teacher's ability to verbalise, i.e. to put into words the experience the children are having, controls much of the use to which this experience can be put, and the children's ability to recall it. The development of mental powers—by which an experience can be re-experienced in thought or built up as sensory imagery—is greatly hastened by a rich vocabulary and the ability to use it. Discussion and the asking and answering of questions is not only remotivating, but good questioning directs observation and makes understanding or misunderstanding more explicit. Children will not experience the world in an orderly, meaningful manner—but a skilful teacher can help the children to perceive relationships, order their experiences and draw meaning from them. The degree to which understanding is present can often influence both the desire and the ability to investigate further, and thereby to learn more.

As the Curriculum Bulletin no. 1, *Mathematics in Primary Schools*, p. 12, puts it: 'Children frequently learn by their attempts to put into words what they are doing, and what they have discovered.'

Multi-sensory stimulation

Adults can accelerate this learning both by provision of a stimulating environment and care in introducing appropriate language at the same time. The more numerous the sensory stimuli, the greater the impact on the recipient (as visual and auditory discrimination are so important in learning to read, chapters 5 and 6 are devoted to their consideration). If it is possible to reinforce the act of seeing with other sensory experiences, such as hearing and smelling simultaneously with the presentation of apt descriptive words, the chances of accurate, vivid concepts being formed is that much greater. This knowledge lies behind so-called workshop-activity-methods. It is quick and easy to teach children, by rote, to give correct answers (both written and verbal) but this sort of learning is relatively useless as it is not likely to be transferred to unfamiliar situations and if forgotten cannot be worked out again. The power to select from your previous experience what is relevant to a new situation, plus the ability to rearrange it and build on it, leads to quick, confident problem solving and original creative thinking. Some information should be committed to rote memory—once it is understood—as this is an economical method of recall. Multiplication takes and number bonds fall into this category.

Practice

Memorisation largely depends on practice—and practice is necessary to fix concepts. It is very important, therefore, that information is accurate and understood before practice takes place. The correction of errors and re-learning can be a depressing, laborious exercise. Modern educational approaches are built on this knowledge, and the motivation required for consistent practice or memorisation of facts like tables comes from an understanding of their usefulness and the economy of knowing an answer without having to work it out each time. This approach can also be applied to the teaching of spelling (see chapter 10) and other useful pieces of information such as scientific formulae.

The refining or sharpening of a concept is the process of generalisation from the particular. The richer and more frequent the experiences of the particular, the quicker the understanding from which to construct a generalisation. Repetition is an essential part of this process and adults must resist the temptation to curtail it. Concept formation may take years and depend upon the assimilation of events experienced many years previously. We also must never forget that as people's mind processes are very different (even when using the same words) we have to make it possible for children to form their *own* concepts, in their own *way*, instead of trying to teach them to acquire ours.

For example, understanding of the commutative laws or of reversibility cannot be *taught*, but is acquired through experience made explicit. Right answers without understanding can only be considered as the ability 'to make the right noises'!

There are three parts to most learning situations: the task, the teacher and the learner. Sound learning results from the fusion of the three parts—the ability of the teacher to communicate with the learner—and of the learner to make clear his understanding of the task. Language is usually essential to this process.

In the writer's view the early stages of learning to read and of studying mathematics are inseparable. Concept formation is necessary not only in connection with the experience but with the words used to describe or recall such experience. The life of Helen Keller demonstrates vividly how the skill of her teacher, Miss Sullivan, made the connection for Helen between the feel of water and the word 'water'. This was the breakthrough into the deaf, blind and hence speechless girl's mind. On this success was built the considerable academic achievements of Miss Keller—including her astonishing power of speech.

Of course it is quite impossible for every human being to discover for himself the sum of human knowledge, and second-hand experiences including verbal description must be used. But parents and teachers have to be sure that a picture or model is sufficiently well understood as being a copy of the real thing—and problems of scale, section or symbolism clarified—or misconceptions and bewilderment can result. This is why it is so important for children to draw/paint pictures and construct models for themselves. These experiences make it more possible for them to interpret pictures, photographs, diagrams and models made by other people.

Referring again to the dog model. Dog-like characteristics can only be teased out from a variety of experiences with dogs of different kinds, sizes and shape. The generalisation will be affected by emotional overtones—whether dogs were nice or nasty, i.e. attractive or threatening; even to whom they belong. The boss's dog, for example, is probably approached rather differently from the stray in the street! The sequence of building a concept will probably include:

(*a*) experience and (*b*) naming (matching with a previous experience) (*c*) recognition and recall will depend on powers of description and comparison (sorting), i.e. degree of similarity or difference, or (*d*) arranging in order of importance (grading) from all of which a personal concept is built.

This concept will be further refined or sharpened by testing one's own *model* of a dog with those of other people, and consequently one's concepts are for ever being altered or remodelled as one is influenced by new experiences or the communicated views of others.

The use of symbols as an economical method of recording and communication must not be hurried. By starting apparently more slowly, we can ensure that symbols are used only with understanding and hence quicker progress and more accurate recording results.

Similarities and differences

Most children seem to notice similarities before differences. A delighted child holds up a scribble for his mother to see and says 'Look! I've made a snake.' To be able to say this he must have had experience of a snake, knowledge of the word and ability to pronounce it sufficiently accurately for his mother's recognition and then to have made a mental bridge between the percept of his wavy line and his concept of snake.

Children play with what lies before them—they do not choose what lies before them. Parents who understand this have contributed greatly to their children's intellectual and language development in the pre-school years. Teachers can only build on what has gone before. A privileged child (and this has practically nothing to do with material wealth) has not only been allowed, but has been encouraged, to explore the world around him; to touch and hold, destroy and build, taste, smell and use every part of his body to feel with. He will have been emotionally and socially supported, so that his pleasure is enhanced, his fear minimised and his confidence undimmed. He will have been protected to the extent of not being allowed to harm himself (e.g. knowing that children pull themselves up into a standing position, tablecloths and handles of saucepans will not be left in his reach, and knowing that young babies learn chiefly through their mouths, noxious substances will be guarded) but safe, different textures will be offered. For most of early and middle childhood, 'Don't touch' means 'Don't learn'. Occasionally the desire to protect young children can lead ultimately to danger, e.g. the gift of a rubber hammer because the parents recognise the need to bang things and naturally do not want the furniture damaged or the baby hurt. Unfortunately these are realistically coloured and accidents have resulted when the child—having formed an inaccurate concept of this shape—uses a real hammer in the same way, or worse, on another child or baby. The same sort of woolly thinking in adults leads to exhortations such as comforting a child who has fallen with 'Smack the naughty floor for hurting baby!' This scarcely helps either to master cause and effect or to sort out what is alive and what is not. Life is quite confusing enough with the indistinguishable differences between dolls which may be abused and babies which may not—or toy animals which can be stepped on or thrown about and cats which retaliate. There are further problems about manners. Food must be eaten from a table at home, but there is a different set of rules concerned with something we call a picnic—or parents are cross sometimes when children do not eat, and equally cross on another occasion when they want to—say in a shop or after being put to bed. Children discover that they may say things when one person is present which cause a great deal of trouble in front of another. Grown-ups can pass personal remarks about children—but woe betide the child who makes a similar observation!

Trial and error learning

All this is part of concept formation and we learn by trial and error
not to comment on similarities and differences which we have
observed—grandpa is *not* pleased to be told his face is as prickly as a
hedgehog, nor grandma to be advised that she is as fat and soft as
uncle's pig; both of which the writer once innocently remarked!

In chapter 2, reference was made to the different aspects of touch
(internal and external sensory stimuli) as well as vision, hearing,
smell and taste. In order to be able to match and sort, children need
to possess adequate physical sense organs—or learn to substitute for
partial or total loss. Children with handicaps need the adults who
care for them to bring the environment to them if they are unable to
move freely about. Time was when this was not understood, and
'institution children' resulted. These children had received adequate
physical care, but had never been able to make the normal close
personal relationship with a mother or mother substitute. As a
result, language did not develop, power to love and make friends was
atrophied and powers of learning were reduced from lack of experience and sensory stimulus. Concepts had not been developed
and even with skilful remedial approaches—progress was minimal
and some children were warped for life.

Play with raw materials

Society is in danger of producing similarly handicapped children if
support is not quickly given to families where housing is not planned
with children in mind, areas of social deprivation which immediately
become areas of educational aridity, from which children come to
school grossly under-stimulated and inexperienced. Much of such
damage is believed to be irreversible. Hence, nowadays, schools
provide many of the raw materials of the world, e.g. water, sand,
clay, wood and living things, bringing the environment to the children which our way of life has kept from them. These raw materials,
which many mothers have neither space nor patience to provide, are
the most essential in helping children's intellectual development.
They have infinite possibilities for exploration and experiment, while
being responsive to the children's sensory equipment they also impose a discipline of their own, e.g. you can't make a hole in water
with your finger but you can in damp sand or clay. Dry sand behaves
in some ways like water, but not in others. You can cut clay up and

join it again, but wood once cut is quite a different proposition.

Closely allied to natural raw materials come the man-made basic materials of paper and paint, chalk, crayon, etc., or surfaces on which these can be used to make temporary marks. Few can resist drawing on the misted pane of glass or the muddy car! Children need long periods of time in which to discover the properties of paint and other marking substances. Experienced viewers can quickly learn much about each child's state of mind, his concept formation, his idea of himself in relation to his environment, human and physical, his readiness for new experiences (of which direct teaching may be one) by sensitive observation and study of his drawings and paintings. It is this knowledge which makes it so vitally important that young children should not be taught '*how*' to draw or paint. Such an action is virtually indistinguishable from trying to teach them *how* to feel and *how* to think and will inescapably result in holding back rather than furthering satisfactory, all-round development.

We all want our children to develop independence and the ability to acquire the basic skills which lead to literacy and numeracy. Such skills depend to a very large degree on a rich variety of experiences— contact with adults who can help such experiences to become explicit and ordered, and adults and children with whom speech is a satisfactory undertaking. The need then both to understand other people's discoveries; to test theirs and your own; and to impart your own, leads to the desire to record and interpret recordings—just as the human race began to discover the means to satisfy such urges a few thousand years ago. People whose curiosity about such recordings is strong are those who engage in the study of civilisations throughout the world, who learn other languages and are still uncovering the diverse ways in which man has sought to impart information both to his fellow men and his gods. The materials which lay to hand were used or fashioned to this end, and their very diversity bears witness to creative thinking. There was no one *right* way. The incised clay tablets and cones of the East, where clay is plentiful and the sun fierce, have a link with the fired pottery, brick and carved stone of our wetter country. Beads in sequences and leather were plaited by the nomadic Red Indian; leather (vellum) was written on with animal or vegetable pigments by using brushes made of animal hair or frayed stems, or pens cut from feathers, bamboo and later metal. Braille, morse-code and shorthand symbols are an extension, adapted to human need; while the invention of cut wooden surfaces, later movable type, the typewriter and the recording machine, accompanied by radio and television, are a further sophistication. The problem is that the need to check veracity and to interpret remains, while reverence for print and unquestioning acceptance is still so strong. 'It must be true, I read it in the paper!' The use of all mass media for propaganda only makes the need to read with a questioning approach (not an unquestioning acceptance) all the more essential.

Summary Play with any material, given time and encouragement, will probably follow the following sequence:

1 Exploration and investigation of the material through the senses, leading to

2 discovery of its potentialities and characteristics leading to

3 experimentation (*a*) this may be destruction or (*b*) construction and need tools in addition to the body.

4 Acquisition of skills and techniques lead to

5 creative use and/or cause and effect use, and/or recording.

Children will rarely, if ever, proceed through any sequence in an orderly fashion—there will be spurts of progression followed by periods of regression. Repetition may be either consolidation or testing, or, with some children for a time, or with most children for a period, an expression of lack of self-confidence demanding reassurance or re-stimulation. The teacher's skill will tell her when to stimulate interest in the next stage *or* another experience with the same material *or* the same experience with a different material.

Making experience explicit through words

Side by side should come the sequence of doing (activity) accompanied by talking about the doing (speech) resulting in clarification through use of words and the emotional support of adult (and perhaps peer) interest, which can usually be contrived to lead into a sharing (recording) experience. The sequence here will be as simple as 'Look what I've made!' through discussion of alternative methods of construction or use; to making an extension or refinement; or adding details to making a book about it; or extending the item into a theme or project, involving other people; or a prolonged expenditure of effort and hence thought.

Summary The teacher is responsible for assessing the stage of development and preparing the environment to stimulate progress to the next. In doing this she must obviously see that the provision and arrangement of material puts neither the children nor the classroom and its equipment at risk. Protective clothing (without trailing ends) for the children and a workmanlike layout of the room, so that materials are visible and sensibly stored goes without saying. Children have to be trained in the use and care of materials and tools. Plenty of time must be allowed for preparation and clearing-up. Much language and mathematical experience can be given through both activities. Progress in social development should come from co-operation and responsibility at these times. The teacher will give a lead, practically and verbally. Her general classroom organisation should be such that her children appreciate order and become able to contribute to it. Standards of layout are usually reflected in the quality of work which results. Let us kill the myth of the artistic temperament being expressed in disorder! A bad workman not only blames his tools but he neglects them and his materials. An attractive, well-ordered classroom stimulates constructive activity and a high level of performance.

Creative activities

These of course result from creative thought, itself the result of seeing a new relationship. This is itself the sum total of matching, sorting and grading activities—seeing similarities and differences and taking the imaginative leap that sees the possibility of a new relationship.

The teaching of techniques, *before* the need for them is understood, may impede, retard or even destroy the ability to work creatively. Technical skill frees the owner to create, because there is no time wasted in management of the medium involved, and ideas can quickly be transformed into concrete forms. Creative use of raw materials depends on the development of powers of discrimination (see chapters 5 and 6), thought and anticipation, and normally, also of language (chapter 1). As we are here concerning ourselves chiefly with children it also follows that creative use of materials depends in schools on the creation of an emotional climate and social environment in which children feel free AND supported in the use of their bodies and other basic material.

Summary Adult comments and expectations must support not oppose healthy growth and development, especially in the emotional sphere. The best guide to natural growth is the behaviour of children untrammelled by adult restraints and the artificial demands of so-called 'civilisation'. Few societies now exist with 'children in mind', for example, how many homes offer all the following aspects of water play?

Water play

(*a*) Grading the tools, containers, etc., that are put ready for the children to use

(*b*) Matching these to suitable water containers

(*c*) Observing carefully

(*d*) Keeping records

(*e*) At a well-chosen moment, talking with the children and asking very carefully planned questions:

> (i) either to provoke thought, or
> (ii) to extend quality of play, or
> (iii) to test understanding

In order to permit play to take place safely and happily, the following preparation is essential:

1 Protection of floor, furniture and child's clothing

2 Warming water—occasionally colouring it

3 Disinfecting
   (*a*) of toys
   (*b*) of water—especially if there is any infection in the classroom

4 Safety, e.g. glass articles only in use when supervised by adult
   metal articles—no cutting edge
   wood—no splinters etc.
   floor not slippery
   N.B. For high-pouring activities make sure the stools/chairs have a non-slip surface and inspect soles of shoes similarly. Usually better to stand behind chair back.

5 Leave plenty of time for clearing-up and provide suitable tools and tanks, buckets, bowls, etc.

6 Adults to empty and fill tanks—hoses useful

7 Provide proper storage for tools to be used in water and plan location of tank, basins, etc., away from activities that water can damage. Ensure that children KNOW what they may and may not put into the water

Types of play in no order of importance

N.B. Stimulate language from the beginning.

1 Body contact with water—as circumstances permit—full experience is desirable:

(*a*) Naked with paddling pool and *fine* spray from watering can or hosepipe. Every form of movement in still and moving water especially jumping and splashing—fresh and sea water

(*b*) Partially naked—legs, arms and face. Finer movements—stir with feet, hands, fingers, etc., stroke and press—saucerful, bucketful—with hand, saucer, ball, stick, etc. Cup hands—pour and sprinkle, etc. Blow at. Make ripples and waves by moving hands below water, etc.

2 Filling and emptying two or three shapes only
Colander: add funnel later
           add tubing later still and/or spoons, ladles
           add jug with lip, kettle shapes, etc.

Repeat by graded containers—narrow necks, etc.

N.B. Containers not too big or weight of water retards wrist control and thumb opposition. Elsewhere give small size cup and saucer and doll's tea-sets

3 Water holders: sponges—cloths and plastic as contrast. Mops with different heads. What sinks?

4 Floaters and sinkers—for older children early classification displays in hoops, trays, boxes, etc. Trick activities like floating needles etc., can sometimes re-stimulate; bobbing for apples

5 Explore possibilities of all types of boat, imaginary, stick or leaf, commercial and home-made. Add sails, fans; use straws and tubes for controlled blowing. Fill until they sink, etc. (see DES and Schools Council 5–13 Science Bulletins re boats)

6 Graded containers which have a relationship but are not named standard measures. Now insist on precise use of language—same as, larger, smaller, full, spill over, empty, half, twice, etc., ref. Piaget's conservation

7 Effect of light on water reflections: apparent bending of stick—rainbows made with spray from watering-can, etc.

8 Ref. coloured puddles in road. What mixes, dissolves or lies as sediment? Shake soil in bottle and watch it separate. Filtering

9 Colander sequence—large holes—small holes—multiple holes—base, side, etc., of containers and in tubes. Watering can, vases and sprays

10 Squeezing tubes to control flow. Balloons, plastic bags, etc., to make jets above/below water level. Water pistols, water wheels, bubble pipes

11 Domestic and dramatic play—waterproof dolls, clothes, washing, etc.

12 Water finding
   (*a*) its own level ⎱
   (*b*) its own shape ⎰ well-nigh infinite progression here

13 Activities with ice

14 Water creatures

15 Rain, rivers and docks, etc.

16 Activities with coloured inks, etc.

17 Activities with wetting and drying—permeability, etc.

18 Standard measures

19 Timing, water clocks, water wheels

20 Domestic play—especially with cooking. Safety?

21 Repeat as many water activities as you can with

   (*a*) dry silver sand ⎱
   (*b*) sawdust ⎰ note similarities and differences

N.B. Sawdust can be dangerous unless supervised—eyes; also clings to clothes. Link wet sand and sawdust with clay, dough play.

The need for first-hand experience

Schools and teachers obviously have to begin where homes and parents leave off. The need for pre-school (i.e. pre-five-year birth-day) education is widely recognised, but since Circular 8/60 (i.e. the freezing of the supply of maintained nursery school and nursery class places in 1960—except for a small extension under the Urban Aid Programme) there has been no increase. The dramatic growth of playgroups is one result, caused by the determination of mothers to 'do-it-ourselves' rather than wait for state provision. A good play-group undoubtedly benefits the children, but it is tragic that so much enthusiasm and goodwill has in some cases had the opposite effect. In the attempt to further the children's development hasty and premature demands have been made on them, including attempts to teach reading, writing and number before the nervous system is sufficiently mature. This is the equivalent of teaching techniques too soon and thus impeding or destroying creativity.

Piaget-type tests are used in schools to back up the teachers' observations. These are intended to discover how the children are thinking rather than to discover how many right answers they have learned. We are much wiser in schools now and recognise the relative unimportance of right *answers* compared with the grasp of understanding *how* they are achieved and hence the ability to work them out again when memory lets you down! The Piagetian stages are a valuable guide to the way in which children should be taught at different stages. Very roughly, Piaget divides chronological growth into a sequence as follows:

Stage 1   0–2 years   Child acquires sensori-motor control
Stage 2   2–4 years   Child extracts early concepts from experiences
Stage 3   4–7 years   Child works intuitively and tests ideas
Stage 4   7–11 years   This is the transitional period between doing things and thinking about them and imagining and memorising what happens.
Stage 5   The last stage is only reached by some people —the period when symbols and abstract concepts are tools with which to think and it is seldom so necessary to return to the handling of materials.

It is fundamentally the acceptance of such stages that has led to diversity of teaching methods in primary and secondary schools, and the recognition that different children will need teaching in different ways.

Summary   Teachers attempt to assess the stage of thinking which children display in a variety of situations (see p. 89, the sheet of matching cards one form of test) and to adapt their teaching and provision of learning situations to such a stage.

Parents can contribute tremendously to their children's chances of acquiring intelligence and developing fully if they support them from birth with warm interest and approval—time and space in which to play with raw materials; if they display interest in what interests the children, helping them to put their ideas into words and listening courteously and uncritically. The need to collect must be recognised and the importance of what may seem rubbish to an adult respected. The 'seeing ear' and 'hearing ear' is of vital importance and shared interests will lead to the development of the children's critical faculties and hence to an increase in intellectual stature.

The ability to match, sort and grade is the gateway to understanding the world around us and the means by which we interpret, understand and in our turn become able to contribute to human progress. Every new relationship envisaged and brought into being is the result of a perhaps sophisticated ability to match similar evidence, sort into coherent groups and grade into a new pattern by selecting and rejecting. No success or failure is displayed when this new relationship is *matched* with the problem which called it forth.

5 Visual discrimination

Bernstein: 'To make the educational experience happy and contented is not necessarily to solve the problems of learning.'

Visual recognition and recall

When we were thinking about reading 'readiness' and symbolism we became aware of how differently we interpret what the physical eye receives, i.e. visual stimuli. To repeat: in order to be put into the position of a non-reader you would have to be deprived of:

(a) years of reading experience, both silent and oral;
(b) the pleasures gained from many types of reading;
(c) the greater part of your passive and active vocabulary;
(d) confidence in your ability to read and make sense of scripts;
(e) the well-nigh reflex left to right movement of both eyes;
(f) and many other aspects of reading skill such as diction, intonation and other expressive techniques.

However, there is one learning situation that can be offered—unknown letters (see the diagram).

Study the explanation and symbols in the first diagram for thirty seconds then turn over and test your ability to read them. If you can do so you have good powers of visual *recognition*, but you probably leaned heavily on similarities and differences noted by comparing these symbols with familiar letters and digits, e.g. ㅂ with B which has a marked similarity *and* difference, or ⌐ᗡ which is intended to have neither.

Without looking again at these symbols, see how many you can write from memory. While you do this, analyse your mental processes: this time you are using another memory power—visual *recall*, but it may be coupled with kinaesthetic memory—the feel of the shape. It may be easier if you keep your eyes shut while you write. If so, can you decide why?

Again, without looking at the original illustration, study the next. Is it the same as the first? If not, in which way is it different? To be

52

able to do this you have to combine visual recognition and recall—
and some people will have to write the symbols, i.e. use kinaesthetic
stimuli, in order to decide.

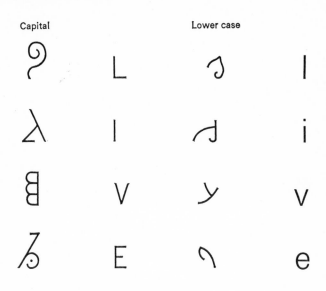

Capital		Lower case	

After thirty seconds, P.T.O.

It is worth while reviewing this exercise in the light of teaching
techniques. In order to have made it easy for you to learn such
symbols it would have been better:

1 to have motivated by giving reasons for learning such words and
building an interest in the verb and adjective spelt 'live';

2 to have presented the symbols horizontally rather than vertically
—so that the visual stimuli agreed with the normal direction of the
letters in a word;

3 not to have presented capital letters which were not to appear in
the test words. This distracts attention from the important symbols
and wastes energy of effort. Note also that the capitals are based on
more familiar shapes—and also on shapes less alike than the lower
case letters, and

4 not merely to have given the meaning, but to have illustrated it
by making it part of a meaningful sentence or story, using the pupils'
passive and active vocabulary. If it could have been linked with a

current classroom interest, e.g. a hamster, the chances of learning taking place would have been enhanced.

What are these words ?

Do not look back

. Same or different ? —

Summary   It is possible to see accurately yet be unable to make 'head or tail of it'.

Part one of the 'triple association'

To consider part one of the 'triple association'—vision.

1 *Vision* We have to *learn* to see

(*a*) physically
(*b*) intellectually
(*c*) emotionally

The human eye takes several years to mature: to co-ordinate with its fellow; to recognise colour and texture, to define movement, to judge distance and size, to select and disregard, to change focus from near to mid and far distance, to interpret: in fact, to discriminate.

Interest heightens visual acuity while fear and pain can temporarily blind one—just as rage can. This is very important, for example, in work both with children and adults on road safety. In 1971 Professor Stina Sandels, working in Stockholm, wrote, 'The fact that the child is listening does not mean that he understands what is being said, even though we ourselves consider the vocabulary to be simple and easy to grasp.' In research with five- to eleven-year-olds, the pedestrian crossing sign was believed to mean that only adults might cross there, while the school sign meant 'Here children must run quickly across the road so as not to get run over'. The writer was engaged some years ago on a survey organised by the Ministry of Transport and a quiz of adults and secondary school children re-

vealed that many of them interpreted ⋂ as being the drawing

of a chimney, meaning built-up area ahead.

We also have to remember that the lower sight level of younger children can lead to lack of clarity and distortion of notices and signs.

A visually stimulating environment

As interest heightens visual acuity we need to provide a visually stimulating environment in schools. On the other hand, the eye tires quickly and an over-stimulating environment will defeat our ends, being either exhausting or soon disregarded. Pictures displayed too long will simply not be seen—another argument for avoiding fixed labels, once believed to teach names of objects. We have to strike the happy medium between enough continuity to ensure security and enough change to stimulate visual attention. Many successful teachers stop occasionally to look at their rooms from the children's point of view: being tall myself it means kneeling in different parts of the room to check what can be seen. 'Out of sight—out of mind' does not always mean a cupboard door or a curtain—it can be equally above or below eye level—or entangled with other competing visual stimuli.

We must also provide materials and activities which will provoke visual attention and by which we can encourage and test the powers of visual discrimination in our pupils. Side-by-side with this visual stimulus must go the stimulus of *meaning* so that attention visually results in intellectual stimulus, and a feeling of satisfaction and achievement.

Classification

A good start is by classifying things—according to colour, shape, size, texture, use and so on. These classifications are discussed and described orally at first and later recorded on labels and statement cards (see chapter 4). Eventually words themselves have to be classified so that they can be used accurately and as effective communication. The same sequence will hold, based on *perception of relationships*. Initially similarity or difference, with words that express these characteristics: same as, not the same as or different, large, small, leading on to larger, smaller, and, as finer grades of classification are understood, *grading* large, smaller, smallest or *seriation* of colour, number, etc., and finally *social and usage* relationships such as sets (in the mathematical sense also) or

families	father, mother, baby
homes	dog and kennel, bird and nest
related groups, such as are used	milk, water, ink or
in Verbal Reasoning Tests	baby, calf, chick

Sequence in 'reading' pictures

Before we ask children to read words we normally expect them to 'read' pictures. The pre-reading stages here are:

1 *noticing* (i.e. a body response to the sight of an object or picture) The baby may point, try to pick up a part of the pattern on a frock or carpet or picture, gesticulate, make a sound of emotion or a facial movement or grimace. We know he has seen something.

2 *naming* The word offered may be correct or incorrect, baby-talk or even a selected sound, but we know that he has linked a visual stimulus with a consistent vocal response.

3 *describing* The content of the picture is described in words, i.e. the visual response has sparked off a verbal response.

4 *interpreting* This is an important intellectual step forward. The previous stage may be simply unlinked words, a sort of inventory, but this stage makes it clear that meaning is being drawn from the picture, and items in it are being related one to another.

5 *adding to—before? after?* This is a more advanced stage, which some children and adults appear never to reach. Inferences are drawn from the picture and the reader can step mentally outside the picture and deduce events which preceded it or are likely to follow.

Obviously we cannot teach through pictures until we are certain that the children can 'read' them. There is also the problem of scale. For example, these illustrations require a vast amount of first-hand experience for accurate interpretation:

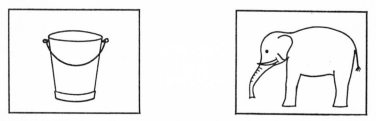

and there is the whole range of graphic styles—from block to line drawings, from full colour to black and white, from representational to abstract, to all of which we are required to respond.

Test scrapbooks

It is with these problems in mind that the writer recommends the making of test scrapbooks. These are complementary to those described in chapters 1 and 2, but, if well planned, can be used in the diagnosis of reading difficulties throughout the primary and secondary school. It usually increases the value if prepared on the scrambled textbook principle—that is—the sequence of pages does not match the sequence of use. It is worth using good-quality paper or card for the leaves—as the book will be much handled. The contents can mostly be cut from newspapers, magazines and advertisement hand-outs. The illustrations are grouped to test some relationship, for example, a page could be confined to food and discussion with a child will reveal whether he can name the food, describe its relevance or even interpret the picture. Other pages will consist of items which have mathematical significance—pictures to match or contrast—cut-outs and insets—different styles of illustration to test visual discrimination sequences such as comic strips—or different letter types—same and different—completion pictures and so on. The children in a class can then be easily grouped by their responses for some direct teaching relevant to them.

Perception of parts of words and letters

When we perceive words, certain parts of words and letters have more importance than others in helping us to recognise words (see the diagram).

The little white rabbit ran away

The little white rabbit ran away

xxe xixxxe wxixe raxxix ran awax

Thx lxttlx xhxtx xxbbxt xxx xxxy

The little white rabbit ran away

THE LITTLE WHITE RABBIT

The little white rabbit ran away

the littl whiet rabbit ran awæ

(i) sentence divided horizontally
    (*a*) bottom
    (*b*) top—the horizon
(ii) sentence without ascenders/descenders
(iii) sentence without other letters, especially vowels
(iv) the complete sentence
    capital letters and cursive scripts provide extra problems for
    many children
(v) sentence in capital letters
(vi) sentence in cursive script
(vii) sentence in i.t.a. (initial teaching alphabet) characters

Summary We have to learn to see physically, intellectually and emotionally—and are aided to do this by interest. The teacher must, therefore, aim for a tension-free classroom, where each child feels he is valued and is making progress, and where the visual stimuli result in meaning.

Part two of the 'triple association'

To consider part two of the 'triple association'—ability to *speak or think* the identified and recognised word *accurately*.

Phonic irregularity

Here we are up against the problem that English is an irregular language and the same letter, or groups of letters, can have different sounds on different occasions,

Note these
eye movements

	name	*sound*
c	see	cease or cat
p	pee	per or ph
t	tee	teh or th

and a left to right eye movement does not always unlock the door to meaning identification.

man   mane

one	bun	bow	bough
gone	?	cow	cough
stone	?	row	through
		mow	although
		sow	lough

The initial teaching alphabet (i.t.a.) is an attempt to present a single character for each of the forty sounds in English, so that a single *sound* can be linked with a single *shape*—dependable and unchanging, thus removing contradiction (see p. 100 for the i.t.a. alphabet and (vii) the same sentence in i.t.a. on p. 58).

Part three of the 'triple association'

To consider the third part of the 'triple association'—the problem of turning marks on paper into sounds and thoughts.

Before we can do this we have to consider the problem of turning noises into meaning, therefore, recorded language, writing and reading, must not be attempted before children have learned to use and enjoy words as speech.

This is not new!

Aristotle: 'Everything that is in the mind was first in the senses.'

Pestalozzi (1746–1827): 'A man must be able to speak correctly and with assurance about many things before he is sufficiently mature to read any book with intelligence.'

Inner speech

We all have a larger passive than active vocabulary, that is, words that we can understand rather than habitually speak. In the early stages of reading children must hear words in order to derive meaning. As time goes on most of us acquire *inner speech*, although it is still possible to meet adults who must whisper to themselves or even just make mouth movements while reading to themselves. Some have to follow their finger moving beneath the words. N.B. It is vitally important, therefore, not to develop habits of finger pointing or mouth movements which may hold back the speed of reading to the speed of hand or mouth movements, whereas the eye and brain can work infinitely faster. Too much emphasis on trying to read silently can result in the development of these harmful reading habits. When inner speech has developed, we no longer need to hear words and speed of reading can greatly increase. The development of inner speech is linked to the physical development of the brain and the nervous system and thus varies from individual to individual.

Span of perception

We need to help children to develop a *wide span of perception*, a good 'eyeful' to reduce the number of eye-shifts per line. If you watch someone reading you can see the eyes move and stop—each movement is called a shift, each stop a fixation, and words are seen only during a fixation. In order to prove how wide your span of vision is, extend both hands in front of you with your index fingers raised. Make a gap of about 1 cm between them. Look straight at this space and without allowing your eyes to move, widen the gap until you can only just see the fingers. This distance is your field of vision— normally much greater than a line of print! With practice (and determination) you can see a whole line in a single fixation. A skilled reader can focus on the centre of a line and read by dropping his eye down the page instead of swinging from left to right across each line, which results in numerous shifts and fixations, or worse still, focusing on a sentence letter by letter! This is the problem for children at the stage where it is so slow and laborious 'sounding out' words, that the grouping of them into a phrase or sentence *having meaning* is not possible. By the time that the second word has been puzzled out, the first has been forgotten! There is the added difficulty of having to reverse the eye movement for words such as mane—where the final silent 'e' alters the sound of the previous vowel. We shall return to this in subsequent chapters on teaching by Look and Say and the teaching of spelling.

Decoding

When the word is finally *decoded* the meaning must be within the reader's vocabulary, either passive or active. A word can be correctly analysed left to right by letter and/or syllable, and the result may yet mask the meaning, particularly at the stage where no inner speech has been developed and words must be pronounced to yield meaning, e.g. picture-sque, past-ry, bib-le. We must, therefore, try to ensure that the words we ask children to read are of interest and within their experience, in order to allow intelligent guessing and re-sounding out. Children must enjoy words and reading books; have experiences that they are eager to share and have opportunities to practise talking and listening, writing and reading and recording in many ways. If words *must* be pointed, let the teacher do so, with a pencil, from *above* the line, i.e. the horizon, and use this pointing to emphasise rhythmical, meaningful oral reading.

Rhythm and stress

Meaning is greatly varied by rhythm/stress. Read this sentence aloud to yourself, stressing each word in turn.

'I am going to post a letter today.'

It is useless to exhort readers to 'put expression into it'. Expression is the result of understanding. Exercises such as the above can often illustrate a reading technique by which the reader can hold the interest of his audience. Probably a better way is to say to the children 'Read that so that I know you are angry, sad, frightened, etc.', and later to ask a successful reader to read aloud to a group 'So that we can all enjoy hearing the story'. It is essential that children are regularly read to—and these readings should be prepared carefully by the teacher, so that as high a standard as possible is offered. It is helpful, too, if the children *see* the teacher preparing and recognise that it takes time and trouble. This both encourages the learner and gives the emotional support of discovering that he merits time and trouble.

Good teachers throughout the centuries have looked at learning problems from the viewpoint of their pupils.
William Bullokar, 1580:

> I did perceyue almost thirtie yeares past, by the very voyce of the children, who guided the eye with the letter and giving voyce according to the name thereof . . . yeelded to the ear of the hearer a cleane contrary sound to the word looked for.
> Hereby grew quarrels in the teacher, and a loathsomeness in the learner . . .

Inglis, 1948: 'The teacher of reading to English speaking children must continue to face difficulties arising from inconsistencies of letter and sound and vagaries of spelling.'

Optical illusions, whether created by conjurors or offered as amusements in the form of drawings, are usually fascinating.

Summary   With reference to the quotation from Bernstein at the start of this chapter, this is true; but in this case it is the obverse: that we do not see accurately when under stress, and if the children are not happy and content it will be that much harder to help them to develop visual discrimination and hence to learn to read.

The initial teaching alphabet

Let us now consider the initial teaching alphabet (i.t.a.) as an attempt to reduce the difficulty of visual discrimination. The i.t.a. is now using its third title. It started in 1950 as the Augmented Roman Alphabet Æ, then became the Initial Teaching Medium (I.T.M.) and is now the i.t.a. (no capital letters). The i.t.a. inventor, Sir James Pitman, is head of a Bath publishing firm, and grandson of the inventor of Pitman's shorthand. i.t.a. is NOT A METHOD, but precisely what it says, an *initial teaching alphabet*. The twenty-six capital and twenty-six lower case letters familiar to us have been replaced by forty-four characters to 'match' the forty sounds of English (see chapter 8, p. 100). There is an explanatory film of this name. No capitals are used—a character is increased in size to serve as a capital. These have been skilfully designed to interfere as little as possible with the horizon in T.O. (Traditional Orthography). Christian names and proper nouns are usually written to T.O.

Sir James Pitman has generously made his invention free to all—claiming no patent—and the i.t.a. Foundation is based at 154 Southampton Row, London WC1. Many publishers now print graded readers and reading books of many kinds in i.t.a. and it is also used overseas especially in the emergent nations. Some local education authorities, notably Oldham, have very large numbers of schools using i.t.a.

Recently the Schools Council commissioned a survey of i.t.a., and this was carried out by the late Professor Frank Warburton and Mrs Vera Southgate in 1969. Three reputable books on the subject by John Downing are: *tꞷ bee or not to be*, Cassell, 1962; *The i.t.a. Reading Experiment*, University of London Institute of Education, 1964; *The i.t.a. Symposium*, NFER, 1967. John Downing led the initial i.t.a. investigation from the University of London Institute of Education, but is now in the United States. (See also the list of general works on i.t.a. at the end of this chapter.)

i.t.a. has been successfully used for remedial teaching of children and adults, such as army personnel.

The writer supports warmly one tenet of i.t.a., that the formal teaching of spelling should be delayed until children are reasonably fluent readers. This is defined by i.t.a. supporters as the time of transfer from books printed in i.t.a. to those in T.O. This transfer is likely to be possible at about Book 3 or 4 of a graded series of reader. Often the same book is re-read in T.O. and the child then continues in T.O. The transition in writing takes anything from a few weeks to a year or more—and is probably speeded by lack of anxiety by the parents and teacher at a mixture of i.t.a. and T.O. in all written work until the 'weaning' process is complete.

It is claimed for i.t.a. that children learn to read faster and with less strain and that accurate spelling is not ultimately endangered. What is usually apparent is a marked increase in creative writing, and, in some areas where the local accent is pronounced—a bilingual child with standard English as an alternative! Most teachers appear to be strongly either pro or anti i.t.a., but the writer hesitates to pronounce either way, having had success in teaching through both T.O. and i.t.a. She has more faith in the Hawthorne effect and feels that teachers must believe in the methods they use if they are to achieve success. Many roads lead to Rome—the teacher's job is to know them all and choose the one that suits each pupil: so that many approaches may be needed in each classroom.

There is one obvious disadvantage of i.t.a. and that is the cost involved in providing reading material which is specialised and meets only one period of school life. This disadvantage is reduced if the local public library supplies large quantities of good quality children's books printed in i.t.a.

It is essential that the school brief the parents as to the reasons why it uses i.t.a. so that the confidence of the parents is maintained and hence the children are not plagued by parental anxiety. Parents need to be quite sure how they can 'help or hinder'.

General works on i.t.a.

Downing, John Allen, *The Initial Teaching Alphabet. Explained and Illustrated* (revised and enlarged edition of *tⱳ bєє or not to be*), London, Cassell, 1965.

The i.t.a. Foundation, *braekthrⱳ in lerning* (Foundation Publication no. 1), London, the i.t.a. Foundation, '5th edition', 1971 (previous editions published under different titles).

Pitman, Sir James and St John, John, *Alphabets and Reading. The Initial Teaching Alphabet*, London, Pitman, 1969.

Pitman, Sir James, *As Difficult as ABC. The case against the traditional orthography as a learning medium* (Foundation Publication no. 4), London, the i.t.a. Foundation.

Warburton, Frank W. and Southgate, Vera, *i.t.a.: an independent evaluation* (the report of a study carried out for the Schools Council), London, John Murray and Chambers, 1969.

Southgate, Vera, *i.t.a. What is the Evidence?*, Edinburgh, Chambers and London, John Murray, 1970.

6 Auditory discrimination

'There's none so deaf as those that won't hear!'

Expectation

In the previous chapter, i.t.a. was referred to as an attempt to represent the forty sounds of English by designing a single character to match one sound, thus removing the complexities of inconsistent spelling. It is, of course, not entirely accurate to claim that there are but forty sounds in English. It was George Bernard Shaw who first remarked that England and America were divided by a common language, and, although we recognise an American accent we are sometimes offended to be told about our English one! With all shades of dialect and accent there are obviously considerably more than forty sounds, though mostly we adapt our *expectation* of sounds and *translate* what we hear into meaning. Here again, emotion enters into the task because anxiety makes it more difficult to hear and retain the thread of conversation or argument. Sometimes we get meaning almost entirely by context or timbre. If you say lovingly 'Come here and I'll beat you!' a dog will come, but he will retreat at 'Good dog!' said truculently. Expectation and deadpan faces are the stock-in-trade of many a comic—and repetition is also used effectively as a vocal joke, our expectation and happy anticipation being skilfully drawn out. The patter song of Gilbert and Sullivan operettas depends as much on the successful and unexpected as well as expected auditory discrimination. Puns and riddles have delighted man through the ages, as Shakespeare clearly knew.

We usually combine facial expression or gesture with words, and maybe give more meaning to the visual and less to the auditory stimulus. Many teachers rely on this for much of their class control and know the importance of the look rather than the word—both of approval and disapproval. We all know the difference between the spoken word and the written (and not just the legal implications as evidence but the ease of interpretation of the former compared with the uncertainty of understanding the latter). We also know how sensitive the blind become to nuances or decibels of sound, in a way that few of us, except perhaps musicians or engineers, can match. For example, the mechanic who explained his bill as consisting of £5 for knowing *how* to listen and 5p *for* listening showed a reasonable breakdown of his skill. It is probable that few teachers give the same amount of time and effort to training auditory discrimination that they give to visual discrimination—just as many of us have been fooled by a correct answer to a sum into thinking that the child understood the process involved. Similarly many children can read aloud accurately without understanding the content—the traditional 'barking at print'.

Importance of being articulate

Man is a social being and needs to communicate. He communicates in adult life mostly by using language and words are the most important units of language. Nevertheless we need to remember that to a young child, speech is a continuous stream of sound, and that the individual words will not be discriminated for a considerable period of time. Even secondary school pupils can make mistakes like 'one sponatime'.

Man alone of living creatures knows how to use words. They give him power over his environment and enable him to manipulate people. The young baby quickly learns to use cries and noises to summon aid, to demand food or to express his feelings. Young babies are frightened both by noise and fear of falling. The unborn child will respond to noise.

In our society the articulate person leads: inspiring reverence, admiration, envy or even fear in his fellow men. Skill in the acquisition, use and selection of words should be a major educational aim—orally as well as written. Literacy is a protection to modern man and few of us can live either happily or successfully without it. We continually make the mistake of assuming that if people *hear* what we say they understand what we are trying to communicate. Some people go still further, believing that if you hear what they say you will agree with it. Equally untrue is the old saying 'Sticks and stones may break your bones but words can never hurt you!' Words are highly emotive and can severely, even permanently, damage a personality. Just as a teacher's expectation is known to have an alarming influence on a child's attainment and learning—so what a child understands of an adult's speech has an equally serious effect. Many a parent and a teacher has made the mistake of discussing a child in his hearing and I had much amusement as a young mother in hearing my four- and five-year-old plotting behind a door, confident that because they could not see me I could not hear them! Just as we must test for the growth of visual discrimination, so we must test for powers of auditory discrimination.

The very young child gets meaning from his emotional and sensory experiences, and gradually has to substitute *thinking about life* for doing and commenting on his experiences. In order to develop his intelligence he must master words and refine concepts. The meaning any one individual associates with a word depends on his own unique experiences—hence meaning varies widely from person to person. It is a basic misconception, to which we all fall victim at times, to assume that the hearer ascribes the same meaning to the words we use as we do ourselves. Comic and tragic misunderstandings result from this precise failure to comprehend the difficulty of 'saying what we mean' or 'hearing what someone else means'. Emotion is at its height when communication is faulty, e.g. a poor telephone line. A friend of mine has a husband who exhorts her 'Don't listen to what I say, listen to what I mean!' a sentiment many of us share, even without putting it into words.

At quite an early age, children recognise the power of words and spontaneous babble and word repetition swiftly become conscious and selective as they test our response. It is odd how confidently we expect children to speak (and they mostly do!) and yet with what anxiety we approach recorded language and how our misgivings are often correct. Anxiety in adults frequently impedes or even prevents progress in children. It is worth recalling that man has been on earth 120,000 years (some experts suggest far longer) and has only recorded for the last 7000 or so. This fact should relieve our anxiety and hold us back from pressurising the five-year-old, or even the 'elderly' seven-year-old, to read and write with speed. After all, many nations do not start compulsory schooling until the age of seven.

'Baby' talk

As well as visual discrimination, then, aural discrimination has to be developed. Baby-talk such as 'free' for 'three' may be due to faulty hearing as well as inability to make correct mouth movements—or even laziness. Faulty sequence such as 'ephalant' for elephant or 'bakset' for basket may be due to undeveloped aural discrimination. Parents and teachers have a responsibility for helping children first to hear and then to imitate accurately. The telling of stories; the learning of rhymes and jingles; skipping and counting games all contribute to the pleasure of words and the understanding of them.

Experiences that excite a need to share them lead to the use of words and finally the need to write them and a desire to discover what other people have written, that is, to read.

Alphabetic method

Time was when adults used the ALPHABETIC method of teaching reading, arguing, logically enough, that as words are composed of letters, children should learn the letters, and, having done this, build them into words. But the irregularities of spelling and pronunciation make this very difficult to do, and we do not hear many letters individually. This last point will be reconsidered in a later chapter—the teaching of spelling—as it is a point frequently overlooked both by pupil and teacher. Even the names of letters are misleading—double 'u' was understandable when the single 'u' was written 'v', but nowadays is obviously difficult for children to understand.

Look and say and phonic methods

The two most usual methods in use nowadays are LOOK AND SAY including word whole and sentence method, and PHONIC. The former depends on choosing words with appeal for children (for preference, those of differing outline and horizon) and then helping them to recognise these in isolation or as part of a phrase or sentence. The phonic approach is more analytical and starts with regular patterns of sounds and/or spelling and more 'drill' on sound recognition and pronunciation of word and letter. This makes for difficulty in interest of content because of the dearth of regular words—though it need not end in the traditional 'the cat sat on the mat' or 'the pig in a wig danced a jig'.

Many teachers use a combination of both methods, starting with Look and Say, following the interests of the children and using their active vocabulary. When some degree of reading skill is achieved, and hence the confidence and motivation of success, then Phonic analysis of regular and later, irregular words is started. This ability to analyse sounds is essential in order to secure independence of attack on unknown words. On p. 81 of the NFER publication *The Roots of Reading* by Cane and Smithers, 1971, we find the following statement: 'We have found it unwise to put absolute faith in a method of teaching reading that is mainly based on only one aspect of perception or communication'. The writer agrees with this view, believing that at different periods, children may switch from an interest and/or ease of response to visual stimuli to more sensitive response to aural stimuli and back again. The diagram of a Homunculus (see W. Penfield and T. Rasmussen, *The Cerebral Cortex of Man: a Clinical Study of Localization of Function*, Hafner, 1968: 'The more a part of the body is used for exploring its environment, the larger is the cortical area') supports the writer's view that the teacher must seek to use multiple sensory stimuli rather than rely chiefly on either eye or ear, and that therefore a combination of Look and Say followed by Phonic teaching is probably the wisest approach to the formal teaching of reading.

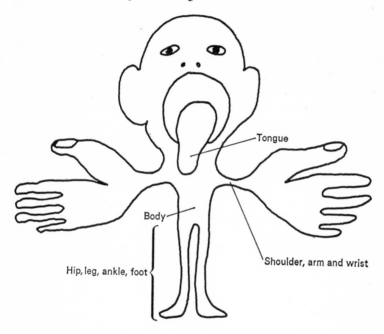

This diagram of a Homunculus indicates roughly the disproportion between the true anatomical size of each part of the body and the relative area of the cortex which responded to electrical stimulation. This should alert us to the need to ensure that children are given the opportunity to explore their environment, particularly with their hands and to talk about their discoveries and interests

However it would be foolish to overlook the increase in confidence and enthusiasm that results when a teacher uses any method or reading scheme in which she has faith and the noticeable surge of interest that accompanies research projects. The Hawthorne effect is a well-known phenomenon. What must be stressed though—and would sometimes appear to be over-looked—is that ability to hear accurately is essential to success in both Look and Say *and* Phonic methods, and, that just as we have to learn to see, so also we have to learn to hear and to listen, and that these are two differing abilities.

Now that 'sweep' tests of hearing are normal practice in nursery and infant schools the high incidence of partial hearing loss has been proven, and many children who in the past would have been held dull, lazy or disobedient have been recognised and given special educational treatment and/or hearing aids. Similarly the vital importance of a good speech model in adults living/working with young children has been recognised, though, in the writer's view, not enough attention is paid in all schools to developing clear and articulate speech, *and* pleasure in using words. It is difficult to find time to listen to children talking, but, unless children receive visual and aural support when they speak, they cease to make progress in this skill and can even regress. In the writer's view this is yet another argument for encouraging parents into school, to talk with and listen to children.

Puns

Humour frequently depends on the similarity between one word and another. There are probably more auditory puns than visual ones. The visual joke is often a drawing (cartoon) though the caption may support the joke—sometimes by being irrelevant. A combination of these puns is found in spelling jokes and some of these may be read as an appendix to chapter 9. The phase when puns and riddles are of absorbing interest to children can be wearying, even exasperating to adults, but the tedium is alleviated when this interest is exploited as a teaching technique.

Swear words

Children are quick to discover the emotive power of words, swear-words especially. In one area where I was teaching, 'cabbage' and 'knickers' were considered by five- and six-year-olds as incredibly shocking—and used in periods of great stress with facial expressions proving understanding of the user's wickedness and breath-holding anxiety of the hearers as to my response.

Anticipatory listening

The fact that the unexpected word makes so much impact—or that we supply the missing word when a speaker hesitates, demonstrates how much of our listening is anticipatory. We expect to hear certain words. Much of our understanding depends on the pattern and rhythm of speech. The foreigner is identified by the rhythm and sequence of words as much as by his pronunciation or vocabulary. Conversely, many people labour under the misapprehension that if they increase the volume of their speech it will be more easily understood by the foreigner. In fact, some adults are guilty of speaking to children in this way with the same aim, or training children only to listen to the third repetition of a request by constant repetition!

Selective hearing

We are selective in our hearing and are accustomed to switching-off certain sounds, e.g. a clock tick or strike, passing traffic or trams; and loom workers can talk normally in weaving sheds and hear each other. Microphones and hearing aids are not selective, and it is important to remember this when speaking to children wearing hearing aids. We can also hear more if we 'attend'. Many teachers have been known to say 'Sit up and pay attention', and assume the latter when they see the former. But hearing is only partly voluntary. Some sounds are physically outside our hearing range: too high or too low; too loud or too soft; unknown, etc. Some are emotionally beyond our reach—frightening, meaningless or boring.

Focus, margin and background of attention

There are three stages of attention—focus, margin and background We can concentrate on attending—make a sustained effort for a short period of time to attend, but not entirely control our listening. If you wish to prove this to yourself, take a blank sheet of paper and write a large A in the centre. Now focus your attention on this, asking a friend to time you for a minute. Few people can prevent their attention wandering—they 'attend' to sounds in their margin of attention and the focus shifts from letter A to the clock ticking, the telephone ringing or even a physical sensation like a tickling hair, the feel of the pencil or a visual stimulus like wondering if the A *is* in the middle of the page, etc. If the supervisory friend makes a remark nearly everyone will attend to it—thus switching from focus to margin. The background of attention consists of those sounds which are normally ignored. These may come nearer to the focus when they change or our emotions are involved. Silence can be more distracting than noise if you are accustomed to noise. Sleep habits are often interfered with by unfamiliar sounds or lack of them.

Interest results in effortless attention and heightened sensitivity of hearing, while boredom and anxiety do the opposite. By the time children have reached school, many of them have learned *not* to hear in self-protection against non-stop radio and television; overcrowded homes and conflicting sound stimuli; lack of interesting sounds and words to attend to; lack of good *two-way* conversation: in fact, they have been bombarded with meaningless or distasteful aural stimuli and learned to disregard them. One of the first duties of the nursery or infant teacher is to make it *worthwhile* for children to listen and later to develop delicacy and precision of hearing, through practice.

Note how we respond to our own names: we can pick these out of a welter of competing noises. We are conditioned to responding to our own names; a problem for the innocent bride as well as the criminal or spy in disguise, who have to learn to respond to a new name, and, even more difficult, *not* to respond to the familiar one. It was an ancient belief that knowledge of a name gave you power over its bearer. Respect for sacred names prevented your speaking them. We all know the response that children immediately give to teachers who can call them by name. Our own names have significance, meaning and interest for us. We are flattered by people who name us after long absence: it gives us status, prestige, importance, a feeling of worthwhileness, of dignity, of welcome—a sense of identity. A good nursery teacher passes a plate of food saying 'and this is for Mary', just as a good mother talks to her baby as she cares for him. Unfortunately many children come to school from homes where the mother does not realise the importance of this aspect of mothering and it is then the responsibility of the teacher to try to compensate: an almost impossible task with the customary large class—and yet another argument for an increase in state provision of nursery places.

Summary   It is essential to hear accurately in order to learn to read. Many children come to school unable to discriminate aurally, and with poor habits of attention. Hearing is only partly voluntary—some sounds are either physically or emotionally beyond our range. Most children can be helped to listen, to attend and to respond.

Training to listen (see chapter 1)

It is generally accepted that the flowering period of speech lies in and around the fourth year of life. Many people believe that children need a vocabulary of 3000–5000 words before the formal teaching of reading should be started. In order to discriminate *words* accurately, we need to attend to and subsequently listen to *sounds* of all kinds. Many people hear more easily if they cut themselves off from visual stimuli (a concert audience with shut eyes) in fact, from all other sensory stimuli as far as possible. Physical discomfort interferes with listening performance.

Very small children enjoy closing their eyes and saying what they can hear. It is a good idea to make tape recordings of familiar sounds for children to identify and name. Dr Maria Montessori valued listening games and used to darken the playroom for the whispering exercise. The directress would go out of the room and call each child by name in a whisper. The child was expected to leave the room silently and join her. Another favourite game is for one child to sit in the centre of a ring of children. As the teacher points to a child he must rise and creep towards the central child and try to touch him before he is heard. It can be most illuminating to discover some children's inability to locate the origin of the sound and point in the correct direction.

All the percussion and stringed instruments, home-made and commercial, are excellent for listening games—matching, sorting and grading sounds for volume and pitch. Montessori bells look identical, but can be arranged in a scale. Children can be encouraged to listen to their waterplay—the sounds made by filling and emptying vessels—using funnels, tubing and straws to make bubbles—hitting water surfaces with flat, clenched or finger-splayed hands—colanders and watercans with roses—jugs and taps, etc. A xylophone can be made with small milk bottles hung from a stick supported on chair backs; with different quantities of water to match the notes of a scale. Falling rain and hail—wind and other natural noises can be noted. High and low sounds; soft, loud, sustained or broken sounds should be recognised, and slowly the children will learn to imitate sounds. As aural discrimination develops, children become sensitive to very small differences and can distinguish between rustling tissue and newspaper—tapping a window with a wax crayon or a pencil—rubbing finger tips over sandpaper or corrugated paper, etc.

Stories, rhymes and jingles, both told and sung, will usually entice children to listen and action rhymes or repetition in stories in which they can take part help in self-control and response to cues. This is a complex form of listening skill requiring memory, anticipation and quick reactions. This all helps children to read aloud meaningfully in due course. Other delights are echo games; imitating and answering clapped rhythms; speaking name rhythms in sequence such as 'Mary, Bob, Penelope, Angela' or 'Rumpelstiltskin', 'Old Mac-Donald had a farm' requires precision and articulation. Rhymes which diminish in sound or word such as: coal truck noises; 'Peter works with one hammer', or even trivialities such as 'Little Peter Rabbit had a fly upon his nose!' excite willing attention, auditory memory and help to develop inner speech. The calling of attention to rhymes, the use of mouth music, crescendo or diminuendo, speaking quicker or slower all help to develop sensitive auditory discrimination. Above all, the teacher must offer a satisfactory speech model—inflection, quality, precision in choice of words—unforced yet faultless diction in their pronouncing.

We need to pay more attention to the connection between movement and speech. Skipping rhymes, counting out rhymes, or ritual rhymes as part of games, we probably take for granted. These follow naturally enough on the heels of 'This little pig went to market' or 'Round and round the garden like a teddy bear, one step, two steps, tickly under there!' but just as we seek to build visual/motor links, so also we need to build auditory/motor links. The good mother counts the stairs up to bed (alas for flats!) and the rhythmical movement helps in memorisation.

Children love to chant multiplication tables to a rhythmic beat. The lullaby is another rhythm and we now have mechanisms to simulate the mother's heartbeats which soothe and comfort emotionally upset babies. Mothers soon learn to recognise the cry of their own babies and can pick this out of a chorus of crying. So also the baby can distinguish his mother's voice and responds at once to it— further examples of selective listening.

If you listen to children at play you will often hear rhythmical humming or chanting of nonsense syllables, comparable to the babbling stage of the baby in his pram. At later stages we *count* in order to help movement: in earlier stages in school it will often be beneficial to *move* to help speech and listening. It has long been recognised that stammerers and stutterers can sing without hesitations or blockages. Encouragement to make sounds or to speak words while moving and dancing pays rich dividends. Formal speech training is probably out of place in the primary school and all teachers are aware that too much correction may inhibit children and thus delay growth of vocabulary and confidence to speak and to question. However, so much of speech development depends on imitation that as much experience as possible is desirable. Listening to the radio, the record player and tape recorder is not only enjoyable but is also giving the children experience which will greatly help their sequencing of sounds and words, which will ultimately help them to read, write and spell. The tiny differences between bill and bell, or pig and pick take time to note and to reproduce. Most children enjoy hearing their voices on a tape recorder and are usually pleasantly self-critical.

Charles Reade (1853–1900) wrote, 'The human craft of writing, which though commoner by far, is so miserably behind the godlike art of speech.'

Without auditory discrimination speech is not possible, and as Piaget noted,

the child does not bother to know to whom he is speaking or whether he is being listened to. He talks either for himself or for the pleasure of associating anyone who happens to be there with the activity of the moment. It is the teachers' responsibility to help him forward to socialised speech [when] the child addresses his hearer, considers his point of view, tries to influence him, or actually exchanges ideas with him.

But we have to do this by enlisting his interest or he will switch-off, demonstrating his boredom as G. K. Chesterton (1874–1936) noted when he wrote, 'A yawn is a silent shout'. Perhaps we should take heart from de la Rochefoucauld (1613–80) who observed, 'We often forgive those who bore us but we cannot forgive those whom we bore', and take advice from E. W. Howe (1853–1937): 'No man would listen to you talk if he didn't know it was his turn next'.

Summary The teacher's responsibility is:

1 To offer a very good speech model—lively, expressive, with excellent diction, inflection and attractive quality of sound. It will be imitated,

2 to listen to the children with genuine interest,

3 to offer a wide variety of sounds to which to attend, including adult and child voices,

4 to give directions and requests once only—after calling the children to attention and giving enough time for them to respond,

5 to remember that 'teaching distance' for very young/immature children is arm's length. Some children *cannot* listen without bodily contact,

6 to use tape recorders so that children can become sensitive to the sound of their own voices as others hear them.

'There's none so deaf as those that won't hear!' but we have to remember that children frequently cannot hear with understanding. The skilful teacher can assess the stage of development of each child and help him towards the next.

R. L. Stevenson (1850–94): 'All speech—written or spoken, is a dead language, until it finds a willing and prepared hearer.'

Susan Isaacs:

> Words are the essential tools of thinking and without them the child's understanding will inevitably be handicapped. Think of the passion of the ordinary child for naming things, and his delight in new words and phrases. Much is going to be lost to the child who has not this fine instrument of knowledge and communication—much of understanding and social experience.

Auditory discrimination allows us to turn *sounds* into meaning.

7   Look and say

'Attention explores—perception discovers'.

In the last chapter, the focus, margin and background of attention were discussed and in previous chapters, the way in which interest heightens the ability to see and to hear. There is no doubt that comics hold attention and are both meaningful and enjoyable. There are now large numbers of comics produced for all ages and some have given a new meaning to the word comic, being designed to horrify; exploit a sordid interest in sex or crime or to cater for readers whose interest in the sensational demands exaggeration both in language and illustration. A fairly recent approach is the comic which claims to be *educational*. Commerce in general has not been slow to discover that the word 'educational' is a best seller, and the most trivial or even dangerous toys can be found to bear this label! Teachers and parents alike will learn much if they study current comics and attempt to analyse their appeal.

Comics

Many of the puzzles offered in comics to young children are, in fact, useful visual discrimination exercises and some demand hand–eye co-ordination skills as well. The use both of colour and different styles of black and white illustration further extends visual discrimination. Hidden objects to be discovered in pictures, more difficult still when comparing block with outline shapes; tangled fishing lines to be traced from holder to catch; mazes; simple picture sequences telling stories from left to right in three or four frames; same and different exercises; visual puns or tracing and colouring pictures and competitions are all excellent pre-reading activities. For slightly more advanced readers there are often spelling games— jumbled letters to be rearranged; crosswords; passages with pictures to be decoded into words or parts of words—verbal puns—alliteration or riddles which all demand attention to be understood.

On the debit side we may deplore:

(*a*) the mixture of classical, magic, science, fantasy and everyday life which does nothing to encourage a firm hold of reality;

(*b*) the vulgarity of illustration;

(*c*) the slang level of language—or degree of Americanisation of words used;

(*d*) the image of parent, and particularly teacher, which is so often derogatory;

(*e*) the flavour of the advertisements, particularly in comics aimed at adolescents;

(*f*) the emphasis on success assessed in terms of money, sex and competition;

(*g*) racial prejudice.

Co-operation seems chiefly described in terms of gang or club and consequent exclusion of those not accepted by the 'in' group.

On the credit side we must recognise the high moral tone of some stories and strip cartoons, and the blackness of the villain contrasted with the whiteness of the hero has respected ancestry in the folk-tale, even if insufficient identification with daily life. There are other social services such as health and grooming articles, dealing with personal hygiene and good eating habits; audience participation in the form of readers' letters or suggestions; helping hand advice sections; correct etiquette or anyhow some tactful suggestions as to acceptable social behaviour while some comics attempt a little real news.

The success of some features is demonstrated by their long life; I possess copies proving that some characters have been living identical lives since at least 1958, and presumably before that? Others are ephemeral and have passed from the pages into memory only. The style of illustration and writing provides immediate identification of the characters and are frequently carefully constructed to appeal to the self-regarding sentiment of children. We are usually well aware of the heroes of the hour, and the attempts of the children to identify with them and emulate them. It is probable, therefore, that we should be wise to give some thought as to how we can compete with comics and transfer their attraction to what we consider more worthwhile reading material. One of the reasons for their success is that they make it possible for the children to get meaning from their pages, quickly and without much effort. Their vocabulary level is low and most words used are in active rather than passive vocabularies. The illustrations and text match each other perfectly. We must not ignore entirely either the added attraction that so many grown-ups disapprove of them! (At the end of this chapter, books and materials specially prepared for children to use in school are discussed and suggestions offered as to angles from which they may be assessed.) How are homes and schools going to compete with comics for their children's attention?

Many schools attach great importance to their choice of a graded reading scheme, and all modern reading schemes have coloured illustrations, and some of them a great diversity of supportive story books, class, group and individual didactic material and apparatus, including discs and filmstrips. Most of these reading schemes offer a teacher's manual which explains the aims of the scheme, the correct use of the material comprising it, and sometimes gives advice on the general philosophy of language development and the teaching of reading. Some schemes are constructed either as Look and Say or Phonic, whereas others claim to be useful to teachers using either method. i.t.a. is not a *method* at all, but a medium designed to be used for early stages of mechanical proficiency and then to be discarded.

The writer believes that for most children a combination of both methods is likely to be effective—starting with look and say, and later building reliable phonic techniques which will make the children confident, independent readers, but that all the teaching should be environmental and draw from individual interests. She further holds that the enthusiasm of the teacher and her ability to adapt her methods to the needs of individual children are all-important, and that most schools will therefore need a variety of reading books to offer to the children and that some teachers (and hence schools) will use no reading *scheme* as such, at all. The reasons for choice must always be based on close observation of each pupil, and an attempt made to use his natural means of learning. Even the alphabetic method will be used if it is helpful—success, achieved with enough pleasure to ensure future reading, is all that matters. There is no *right* method of teaching reading—in fact, some children appear to need no 'teaching' at all, but these are the favoured few, for whom the environment was perfectly 'prepared' whether by intent or chance.

Pre-reading programme (i.e. the preparation)

When the children come to school for the first time, the teacher will immediately start to assess their readiness. Her records will display her skill in sensitive and comprehensive observation and, as well as assessing the present state of readiness, she will be doing all she can to stimulate further stages of readiness. Obviously the influence of the home is paramount and the experiences the children bring with them will range from a full, rich verbal background to a severely deprived one. The pre-reading programme will therefore have to cater for many different levels.

By far the most important is to establish a classroom atmosphere in which the children are at ease and in which they are stimulated by every sort of sensory experience and the need to talk about it and share their impressions, feelings and ideas (see chapter 2).

Stories read and told

Probably the two most effective ways of motivating children towards reading are (i) story-telling and story reading and (ii) making books with them.

(i) *Story-telling* has always been one of the ways in which the culture has been passed down from generation to generation—and great teachers have always used it as a method of instruction. The parables of Jesus, the myths and legends of all nations, the fables of Aesop, the stories collected by the Brothers Grimm, invented by Hans Andersen or la Fontaine, nursery rhymes and *Gulliver's Travels* (often far removed from childhood in origin) right up to modern times and the joys of Edward Lear, Beatrix Potter, Lewis Carroll, the Farjeons, and thousands more too numerous to mention, have all informed us about ourselves and drawn us from ego-centricity towards the understanding of other people and considera-tion for them. All teachers of young children need to be able to tell stories—to enjoy watching the faces of listeners and sharing with them the tale that suits the occasion. Many teachers invent simple stories about the children themselves or their immediate environ-ment that help them to live in it with understanding, just as in civilisations past, man sought to master his fears by inventing explanations of natural phenomena. Good story-telling helps children develop the power to listen—and some stories which invite partici-pation like 'The Gingerbread Man', the 'Three Little Pigs' or 'This is the house that Jack built' can lead to good speech and self-control too.

When stories are read, the book needs to be held so that the child/children can see the pictures and print. Attention must be drawn to the print, so that the children begin to recognise that this is *visual speech* and that when you can read you can turn these marks into sound and sense. We must take special care to help the children to break up the continuous stream of sound—which is speech—into its component parts, the words. Probably the easiest single word to disentangle is a name, not least because of its emotive value. Goldilocks is a word that is fairly easy to isolate in a few lines of print, and some children enjoy searching for Goldilocks among a number of flashcards including their own names and those of their friends. This sort of game can be used as an extension or introduction to a story—but the teacher must consider whether this could destroy the emotional satisfaction of the story itself. Sometimes children can only listen to a story in a one-to-one relationship and must be seated on the adult's knee before they can attend. These are the situations where extra adults are so welcome in school—the head or a part-time teacher, an ancillary such as a general or nursery assistant—or parents who can make themselves acceptable in school, working under a teacher's direction so that they really support as they intend to, and do not impede the work going on. It is the rare child who can continue to behave naturally when a parent is in the room with his teacher. There may easily be a conflict of loyalty, or an expression of jealousy if his parent gives attention to other children. Many schools and parents have overcome this problem by arranging that parents work with a different class. Parents have also dealt most successfully with other language situations—such as helping children to cook, thus releasing the teacher for areas where her technical expertise is essential.

(ii) *Individual home-made books* Another pre-reading situation that is vitally important is the making of individual books. These may well be constructed from the drawings and paintings of one child—and the text will be written *in his presence and at his dictation* by the teacher or ancillary. Other books may be made by the teacher for an individual child, using a known interest or emotion, perhaps such as to help the older child to readjust to the arrival of a new baby. By diverting emotion from resentment to protection and shared responsibility—'Johnny's baby sister'—the twin needs not to feel ousted and also to put feelings into words can be met, and the proud owner will spend quite a lot of his time taking *his* book about *his* baby around the school. The adults will all recognise the need to build up his own confidence by sharing his pleasure in his book and commenting on his good fortune at having a new baby—'his' baby—at home. Parents can sometimes help older children to look forward to the birth of a sibling by telling stories, discussing the provision of a cot, etc., at home, and making a fuss of the older child so that he does not feel less important—but more. We do not always remember how long it takes to be able to share. There is all the difference in the world between agreeing to hand over one's cot to the newcomer 'because the baby is so small' and then adapting to the new bed as a pleasurable event: 'Daddy got it for me, because I am so big!' rather than 'You'll have to sleep in a bed now—because I need the cot for baby!'

Stories allow children to re-experience and re-think events without personal involvement. They foster the ability to put yourself in someone else's shoes and hence to move out of egocentricity (NOT selfishness, but unawareness of others) towards a sympathy and a feeling towards others, and a slow recognition of their similarity to yourself. What did it feel like to be each person in 'The Tale of a Turnip'? or 'Little Black Sambo and the tigers'? or Milly-Molly-Mandy? We need to be very careful that we do not tell fairy stories before the children have sorted out fact from fantasy—for the warm security of *let's pretend* can give way all too easily to the cold terror of fearing that grandmother could turn into a wolf! We all know the bear under the bed is quite smart enough to go away when Mummy looks, but he sneaks back directly she goes downstairs—especially if the light goes out before the child is mature enough to welcome darkness. Stories should comfort and amuse, not chill and frighten.

The approach to Look and Say centres on

(*a*) the increase in vocabulary and the pleasure of conversation, i.e. speaking AND listening;

(*b*) the realisation that writing and print are recorded speech;

(*c*) the slow ability to hear speech as separate words rather than a stream of sound; followed by

(*d*) the skill of recognising words in their visible form and relating them to the sound of the word spoken by others or oneself—and the meaning of the word.

Classroom activities for word recognition

1 *Use name cards*—lettered in lower case letters (height of 2 cm) Jonathan not JONATHAN

    (*a*) recognise own name
    (*b*) match—same as
    (*c*) sort—different from
    (*d*) grade by long, short, e.g. Goldilocks contrasted with Tom
        longer, shorter
        ascenders and descenders
        initial letters

(*e*) Play games such as distributing cards round the room. Each child finds his own name and sits by it. Later, as sight vocabulary increases, other forms of treasure hunt are enjoyed. Children can hide cards for each other. The finder has to read the card and say where it was hidden.

(*f*) Postman. Distribute cards as if they are letters.

N.B. 100 per cent success is desirable, and children enjoy inventing their own flashcard games.

2 *Room labels* for material storage, job charts, clothes' pegs, models, pets, etc. Start with symbol and word

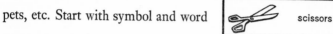

Later remove symbol and introduce change in scale—requiring

scissors to be matched with **scissors**

N.B. remember to use cards which allow a good margin round all letters (usually the height of a lower case letter 'a') for ease of visi-

bility, = **peg** not **peg**

and later to have identical size of card so that the children have to read the word and do not select the word by length of card.

3 *Statement cards* (see chapter 4)

4 *Command cards* These carry commands to perform certain actions: Stand. Clap. Open the door. Fetch a bottle of milk, etc. In the early stages the length of sentence may well be a cue. As with single words such as Goldilocks and Tom above, the grading eventually compels reading, not shape/length recognition.

5 *Children's own paintings and drawings* These are labelled, while the owner watches. The legend can be just his name 'So that I will know it is yours' or, as the content becomes intentional and symbolically representational the words can relate to the painting. N.B. the value of repetition and reinforcement.

6 *Individual books* The motivation is based on acceptance of egocentricity. 'My Book' implies that I am a worthwhile person, my work is important and valued. I can read my name, Daddy, Mummy, etc. The child feels a growing sense of power over his body, his environment, his ability to understand and share, i.e. '*You* look at *my* book, *I* look at *yours*'. There is complete absence of competition in the sense of hurtful comparison—and much experience of approval and success. There will be maximum association of the spoken and written word with satisfying activities, which will lead to a desire to

repeat them. Activities can be recorded that are dramatic, physical, destructive, constructive, that deal with people and things or recall known situations or familiar places.

Key words and context

7 *Key words* The important words must be selected in sentences and the 'filler' words (the, and, was, etc.) given less attention. Here again, personal involvement is a good start. David brings a coloured leaf, which is displayed with a label 'David brought this red leaf. He found it in the park.' Questions such as 'Who brought it?' 'What did David bring?' 'Where did he find it?' 'What colour is it?' 'Can you find another red object?' 'What else is the same red as David's leaf?' will direct attention to such words and their relationship to each other which eventually leads to expressive reading.

8 *Words must be recognised in any context*, different scale and eventually different type. At first it is wise to keep all classroom and other flashcards, statement and command cards in uniform lettering, but as skill and security grow the same word must be presented in different forms, so that the *meaning* is matched, not its visual form. The aim is to build the 'triple association' of sight, sound and meaning, wherever possible.

In early stages a copy to carry and hold next to or below the other word is essential. As visual memory develops, the matching can be done by recognition. Eventually recall permits a child to write the word correctly without a copy.

Later still parts of words can be matched—initials (single letters or digraphs), endings and finally middles. It is important not to call attention to ends and middles of words before left to right eye movement is habitual. As soon as possible, train the children to guess the word from the context.

Verbalisation

Throughout the day the teacher must verbalise, i.e. put into words the experience the children are having, and coax them to use such words in their conversation with her. She must also seize opportunities to draw attention to the written word, its relation with speech and its use, e.g.

'I'd better write that down then I'll remember.'

'Please take this note to Miss Smith. It asks her to lend us some glue.'

'Please give this letter to Mummy—it asks if she will let you come to the zoo.'

(Looking at a named article) 'This belongs to John. It has his name on it.'

'I don't know (even if she does!). Let's look in this book and find your flower's name', and so on.

'Read and do' cards

Commercially produced cards can, naturally enough, seldom meet the need of the moment. Children's interests are unpredictable and the verbal content of a 'Read and Do' card will need to be chosen to match each child's ability and skill. In early days the teacher will need to prepare cards, but as the children become more able to write they delight in inventing cards for each other. This results in a lot of most desirable repetition and re-reading—as the author has to check his friend's response. Children who have enjoyed some task—perhaps making bread—like to write out their accounts in the form of recipes or instructions so that other children can try too. Family grouping makes this sort of approach very easy—and leads to co-operation and support of each other rather than to the aggressive criticism which too often results from competition.

Use of graded reading schemes

Many children are taught to read without a graded reading scheme or by using books from several schemes. This is probably ideal in that the work will be based on the children's own experiences and interests. However, the teacher must select with care and not confuse books based on a Look and Say approach with those written for a Phonic method. For less experienced or less confident teachers, a good reading scheme is a support and hence to be recommended. It is vitally important that no scheme should be used without a thorough study of the teacher's handbook. This is not just a normal courtesy to the author but an essential preparation to using the scheme intelligently and ensuring that books and apparatus are presented and used as intended.

It is generally accepted that approximately 80 per cent of people use a predominantly visual approach to learning, being more sensitive to visual rather than auditory stimuli—but all people learn more quickly and effectively when receiving multiple rather than single sensory stimuli. Therefore children will benefit greatly from kinaesthetic stimuli resulting from writing—and should be encouraged to trace and copy words which they are learning to read at sight (see chapters 5, 9 and 10).

Word counts

Numerous word counts of children's spontaneous speech have been made—and some of these have been used as a basis on which to build a reading scheme. In the past there has been a tendency to drill certain words, to ensure that children can recognise them on sight. It is certainly tempting when one is told that these following twelve words form a quarter of all words in the average English book, viz: a, and, he, I, in, is, it, of, that, the, to, was, and that these twenty added on form one-third: all, are, as, at, be, but, for, had, have, him, his, not, on, one, said, so, they, we, with, you; while if we embark on learning only a hundred we will know about half of all words used in the usual everyday books and newspapers. However, if you look at these words, they are chiefly filling-in words, with little intrinsic interest. All these above words lie in quite young children's active vocabulary and are used with assurance, but teaching their meaning out of context, let alone making the children *want* to learn them, is quite another matter! In my experience they are learned quickly when needed in writing and can be practised without boredom or lack of understanding in phonic drill, word-building and spelling (see the following list).

Most used words in English *

List A (12 words make up, on average, one-quarter of all reading)

a	and	he	I	in	is	it
of	that	the	to	was		

List B (20 words; with List A makes up one-third of all reading)

all	as	at	be	but	are	for
had	have	him	his	not	on	one
said	so	they	we	with	you	

List C (68 words; with Lists A and B make up one-half of all reading)

about	an	back	bee	before	big	by
came	can	come	could	did	do	down

* From *Key Words to Literacy*, McNally and Murray, Schoolmaster Publishing Co. Ltd, Derbyshire House, St Chad's Street, London, WC1H 8AJ.

from	get	go	has	her	here	if
just	like	little	look	made	make	more
much	must	my	no	new	now	off
only	or	our	other	out	over	right
she	some	well	them	then	there	this
up	want	their	went	were	what	when
which	who	will	your	call	first	into
me	old	see	two	where		

List D The next 100 most used words

after	again	always	am	another	any	ask
away	bad	because	best	bird	black	blue
boy	bring	day	dog	don't	eat	every
far	fast	father	fell	find	fly	five
four	found	gave	girl	give	going	good
got	green	hand	have	head	help	home
house	how	jump	keep	know	last	left
let	live	long	man	many	may	men
mother	Mr	never	next	once	open	own
play	put	ran	read	red	room	round
run	sat	saw	say	school	should	sing
sit	soon	stop	take	tell	than	too
these	thing	think	three	time	tree	under
us	very	walk	white	why	wish	work
would	year					

50 additional nouns

apple	baby	bag	ball	bed	book	box
bus	car	cat	children	cow	cup	dinner
doll	door	egg	each	farm	fish	fun
hat	hill	horse	jam	letter	milk	money
night	nothing	picture	pig	place	sea	shop
sister	street	sun	table	tea	today	top
train	toy	water	morning	Mrs	name	rabbit
road						

These 250 words make up approximately 70 per cent of juvenile reading and about 60 per cent of adult reading.

It is certainly important that the greater part of all the important words, i.e. the key words, are known before children embark on attempting to read a book. The teacher usually ensures this by a period of story-telling and discussion of pictures—which not only motivate interest-wise, but result in the necessary words being learned by sight. Most commercial schemes have large pictures designed to stimulate such conversation. Another useful teaching aid is the flannelgraph, cellograph or magnet board, on which both teacher and children can rearrange figures and articles while telling a story or recounting real-life events. This is a useful midway step between enacting an event and reading/writing it in a book.

Picture dictionaries are also useful in linking word shape and meaning, provided that the children can 'read' the picture. Preferably they are made with individuals or groups of children, but it is sometimes difficult to combine a high standard of display lettering with classroom activities. One way is to prepare well-lettered labels in advance—write the word while the children watch and then substitute the fair copy version and stick it on to the chart.

Matching cards

These can be made both as self-corrective teaching material and as test situations. Children can enjoy them and voluntarily spend quite long periods of time playing with them as puzzles. Commercial ones can cost rather more than many teachers feel like spending, but with forethought equally useful sets can be made for comparatively little outlay. Cards slightly smaller than standard playing cards are suitable and can be quickly cut in large quantities by a guillotine. Alternatively some printers will sell quantities of unprinted tickets in a wide range of colours, and these are often no more expensive but beautifully precise. The major sequence is normally:

(*a*) colour
(*b*) object
(*c*) shape
(*d*) picture and word or digit
(*e*) word alone

but each stage can well be subdivided.

Five pairs per envelope is enough for most young children as a start—but some children like an even larger range to sort.

(*a*) *Colour*

(i) 5 pairs of strong colours
(ii) 5 pairs of pastel colours
(iii) 5 pairs of one colour, shaded from dark to light

(*b*) *Object*

    (i) 5 pairs of toys, animals, furniture, clothes, vehicles, etc.

    (ii) 5 pairs of objects in different scales—match large doll to small one, etc.

    (iii) relationship pairs—match cup and saucer; egg and egg cup; bird and nest

(*c*) *Shape*

    (i) obvious regular shapes—circle, square, triangle, etc.

    (ii) same shape to be sorted by colour—red, yellow, green, blue, black circles

    (iii) irregular but well defined shapes

    (iv) much more similar shapes

    (v) block and outline

(*d*) *Picture and word* (digits)

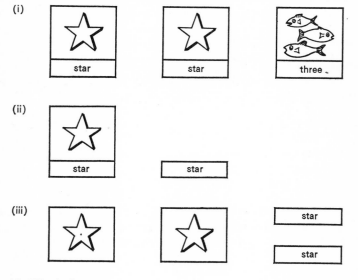

(*e*) *Word alone*

For teaching purposes the cards can be made self-corrective by cutting them in patterns.

This ensures that they can only be fitted together correctly. The same method can be used with jigsaw sentences—and a pattern or colour along the back helps for quick sorting out by the teacher.

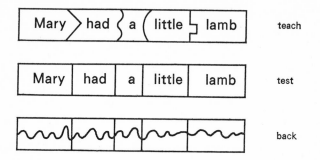

Finally, words can be broken into parts also. It is usually wise to break at syllables.

Bingo or housey-housey games

These are a variation of matching games which can be used by children on their own or in groups. When used for groups, ensure the words are arranged in a different place (see above).

cat	down	stool
their	mother	home

home	cat	mother
down	stool	their

To be sure that each set matches, make two cards at a time, overlapping one slightly while lettering. Then cut one card up into separate words.

Labelled pictures

Another useful matching game is to prepare labelled pictures—ideally two of each illustration.

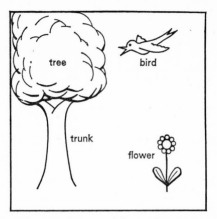

Teaching On the first picture stick words or arrange them on the mount with lines to the objects. Provide a duplicate set to match.

Testing Offer the same picture with the loose words only. An envelope on the back of the mounted picture can be used for storing loose words.

Children working in pairs will talk about the picture as well as learning the words.

To ensure standard size of name cards, or other desk material it helps to cut a template

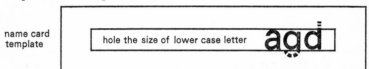

A very sharp 3B pencil will give such light guide lines that new bread will remove them without damaging the lettering.

There are almost infinite varieties of bingo games—the full range of matching cards as already listed. After that words can be matched and also paired—capital letters and lower case; different sizes; relationships such as cow, calf, hen, chick, or bird, nest; dog, kennel, or milk, water or 5, five, etc.

Other useful visual discrimination games are the (A) odd man out or (B) nonsense variety.

(A)

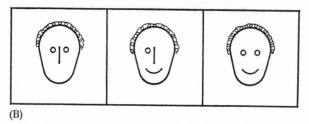

(B)

These lead to interesting conversation situations and at later stages, the children like to write about such drawings and invent others.

Jigsaws

Useful desk material can be made from old Christmas cards which have been glued firmly along the fold. These can be cut into pieces—both self-corrective and test—and the intricacy of cut and detail of the picture control the grading.

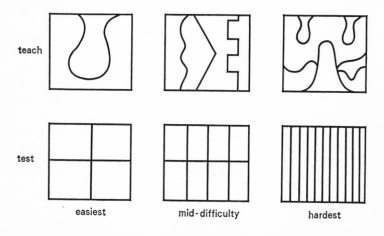

teach

test

easiest   mid-difficulty   hardest

Matching card alternatives

These are used both to help children develop visual discrimination and to test how far their discrimination has developed.

There are five major stages:

1 Colour   2 Shape
3 Picture   4 Symbol and Picture
5 Symbols alone

These stages are subdivided, and fine grading can be offered.

1 *Colour* At first strong colour contrasts are distinguished—red, blue, yellow, black, white. Later shades and tints are recognised. Colours are also attached to objects and pictures, a red ball, a blue train, etc.

Use dominoes, lotto cards, fabric and threads, etc., as well as formal cards.

2 *Shape* Similarly—begin with strongly contrasted shapes, e.g.

(*a*) square, circle, triangle, oblong, star
(*b*) progress to shapes very similar in quality and finally
(*c*) outlines—both matched with each other and
(*d*) harder still, with the block shape of which they are the outline

i.e. split a group of (*b*) and (*c*) and combine to make stage (*d*)

3 *Pictures* Pairs of pictures, at first bold and coloured and later progress to black and white outline drawings

Use commercial dominoes and lotto as well, but these are expensive compared with those you make yourself. See catalogues, advertisements, etc.

Parallel with this level go the cards for digits and numbers, i.e. verbal and numerical symbols

(*a*) picture and word written below it or figure written below it
(*b*) picture + word, and another loose card with the same word/figure on it
(*c*) picture alone + loose word/figure, or spot notation and cards with pictures on

4 Pictures with a number of words to be placed in the correct place. Use also flannelgraph, cellograph, etc., material

5 Words and sentences alone

(*a*) Sentence to sentence (plus a picture if necessary to give a clue to meaning). Otherwise start with known rhymes, and lead into new testing material
(*b*) Sentences + loose words
(*c*) Words alone

Much later when phonics are taught

(*d*) Sentences cut into syllables

Later still when spelling is taught, words cut into letters.

Jigsaws These are used simultaneously, and are graded by picture style and cutting.

Start with few pieces—cut to be self-corrective, and work on through more pieces and more complicated cutting to adult standard jigsaws.

Commercial material:

(*a*) insets into which only one piece will fit (pictures)
(*b*) geometric shapes, usually graded in size
(*c*) fractional parts
(*d*) interlocking

These are expensive and many stages can be home-made cheaply —see examples displayed.

In earlier chapters the writer suggested that the early stages of learning to read and of forming mathematical concepts was identical. Obviously, before engaging children's activities with two-dimensional material and symbolic representation, a great deal of matching, sorting and grading has taken place with real objects and later, miniatures and models. Statement cards provided by the teacher will give place to those written at the children's dictation and later still those written by the children, as need demands. Every sort of classroom activity has verbal possibilities, and the teacher must sense how far to take these in terms of recording. Just as we recognise the pre-verbal conversation, so we recognise the need to do without either talking or recording. The sensitive teacher does not intrude on the children when they are trying-out ideas or exploring or experimenting in the very early stages. The concentration is clear on the children's faces and must not be broken. It is in family grouping and integrated day organisations that it is easiest to provide such privacy and individual learning situations—but the determined teacher can contrive a degree of individual freedom if she recognises its importance. There is a place for class, group and individual learning and teaching on different occasions and careful observation, record keeping and a willingness to try out a different way of work will safeguard children's differing patterns of learning and rate of development.

Summary As English is an irregular language many words cannot be analysed phonically. With an alphabet of twenty-six letters it is obvious that the major forty sounds of English cannot be accurately represented. It is clear therefore that many words must be acquired as sight vocabulary.

The advantages of a Look and Say approach means that there is no restriction on vocabulary—and any word within the children's passive or active vocabulary can be presented. If the teacher is skilful and the children 'ready to learn' and 'willing to be taught', confidence can be established in the reading situation by building a sight vocabulary of a few hundred words. Similarities and differences must be emphasised but more stress laid on meaning, e.g. irregular words such as once, aisle, gnat, knight, lamb, said, who, two, or those with more than one pronunciation: read, live, either, must be learned by sight but the visual similarity of regular words can be quickly linked to phonic similarity and on this foundation phonic skill can be built: a necessity for independent attack on new words.

Choice of reading books

In order to help the evaluation of reading books some of the following questions might be posed.

1 Does the material pre-suppose a particular *method* of teaching reading?

2 Is it a *graded* reading scheme? If so,

    (*a*) What grading is involved? e.g. Look and Say or Phonic or parallel sets of readers?

    (*b*) Controlled vocabulary?

    (*c*) Is the type-face slowly reduced in size?

    (*d*) Are the illustrations graded in visual complexity?

    (*e*) Are there supplementary readers?

    (*f*) Are there work books?

    (*g*) Are there any other pieces of apparatus?

    (*h*) Are there record cards?

3 If it is based on *Look and Say* (word whole or sentence approach) does the vocabulary used approximate to the passive and active vocabulary of the children you teach? What is the pace of the introduction of new words?

4 If it is based on *Phonic* approach—do you accept the sequence of sounds that have to be taught? What auditory discrimination is demanded?

5 If *colour* or *diacritical* marks are used as cues what level of visual discrimination is required? How is this to be assessed? Do you know which of the children you teach has impaired colour vision?

6 For 'specialised' schemes—do you understand and accept the philosophy underlying this series?

7 Consider critically the *format*, *layout* and *construction* of the books—especially in relation to the price, e.g. cover strength; stitched or stapled (if the latter, is it worth stitching and reinforcing?); quality

of illustration and relevance to text; type-face and size of type; spacing of words and rows to aid vision; paper quality and strength; proportion of papers and margins, etc.

8 Are the books attractive:

(*a*) full cover
(*b*) spine
(*c*) size, shape and weight to the children who will handle them?

9 Does the story content appeal?

N.B. Social and emotional level of readers; interest age; local environment; home conditions; vocabulary (passive and active); experience to support stories, reality or fantasy; cultural familiarity or ignorance, etc.

10 Is the book/apparatus likely to meet the children's needs and motivate them towards other reading and writing activities?

Finally I suggest that for many children the most valuable books are those made by teachers and/or children—for these can record experiences, ideas and discoveries in a way that ensures understanding and pleasure. It may well be that the making of a book is one of the experiences that leads children to value books and handle them with respect. Surely it is therefore of the utmost importance that we choose wisely (with special reference to the *quality* we put before the children) the books we use when we attempt to teach children to read?

8 Phonic methods

Child: 'Do you know what a step hen is?'

Problems of English spelling

George Bernard Shaw gave another example of the problems facing the would-be reader in his plea for reformed spelling. His example was 'ghoti' and the unwary will read this as 'goatee'. However the word also stands for 'fish', i.e. gh as in cough, o as in women and ti as in station. The child who asked me what a step hen was had applied correct left to right eye movement, his ability to group letters into meaningful known words step and hen—but this was not enough. He may well have been aware of the 'ph' digraph, which appears at the beginning of the word 'phonic', but did not recognise it placed halfway through the word. 'Stephen' is probably learned more easily in Look and Say, because the left to right analysis may easily result in step hen. There are therefore two major aspects of teaching phonic analysis that must be borne in mind:

(*a*) the irregularity of spelling and sound values given to letters in the English language;

(*b*) that left to right analysis cannot unlock the meaning from other cues as well, the main one probably being context. This brings us once more to the value of an extensive vocabulary—an interest in words, confidence in being able to express ideas in speech and gain meaning from other people's conversation—all of which many children acquire effortlessly in the home where parents talk with their children, tell them stories and share books of all kinds with them (see chapter 7).

Teaching reading by spelling (see chapter 10) or the alphabetic method: Keh-ah-teh = cat (which it obviously doesn't! Test yourself and speed up the keh-ah-teh and you still do not reach cat) is sometimes wrongly called a phonic method. A truly phonic method is the teaching of letter sounds individually, later digraphs such as 'ph ch th cr st sh', etc., and building these into words and finally sentences. Most phonic reading schemes combine this approach with some preliminary visual work.

Another confusion arises from the fact that many people use *phonic* and *phonetic* interchangeably. There are several different versions of attempts to design symbols which isolate the individual sounds made by mankind in his divers languages. Many of us have enjoyed the dramatic use to which this technique was put in *Pygmalion* or its film version, *My Fair Lady*. There is an international phonetic script, used in pronunciation dictionaries, which goes most of the way in offering a notation (such as music) which has universal acceptance. Shades of dialect can be recorded as well as the different sounds comprising living and dead languages. However, this is not a method of teaching reading.

Alphabetic approach

In the recent past many children were successfully taught to read by alphabetic (spelling) methods, but in general these have been abandoned because of the degree of rote teaching and hence 'drill' required, and the generally accepted view that children learn best when their work has meaning and intrinsic interest. In order to build the new on the known, the vocabulary had to be limited, and readers were full of sentences such as

'The cat sat on the mat'
'The pig in a wig danced a jig'

from which it is extremely difficult, if not impossible, to build interesting stories. If we analyse 'the cat sat on the mat' it can readily be seen that the children had to differentiate between three curves

c   s   m

on a very small scale. c is the top half of s and m is made of two c shapes, joined and turned through 90°. In chapter 5, attention was called to the slow growth of visual perception and the ability to distinguish between inversions and mirror images. The logical inference that if you can read 'cat', then 'sat' is an easy extension, overlooked the fact that major differences are easier to see than minor ones—and 'aeroplane' and 'cat' are easily distinguished, but 'cat' and 'sat' easily confused. Equally 'cat' and 'sat' require careful listening to be perceived accurately while 'aeroplane' and 'cat' are easily kept apart aurally. Finally—and by no means least significant—the meanings of 'cat' and 'aeroplane' offer more exciting possibilities for stories than cats and mats! We can therefore, with more assurance, expect the children to be better motivated towards their reading material if it can be constructed to match their interests and environment. The alphabetic method of teaching reading came into favour at the period of payment by results. When the idea of paying teachers according to the performance of their pupils was explained in parliament the merit of the scheme was that if it were not efficient it would be cheap. It *was* cheap! Teachers were compelled to ensure that as many of their pupils as possible reached the minimum standard required, and learning by heart all too often replaced the ability to read the text. Equally the more able children tended to be held to the level of the least able.

An obvious result of such mechanical teaching was the need for punishment to maintain effort, and the cane was part of the teacher's equipment. Even Maria Edgeworth, a very liberal-minded teacher, saw nothing amiss in teaching reading with the Bible and a thin rod. The link of the rod and education was at one time so pronounced that university students were compelled to submit to public floggings. Even today there is still widely held support for corporal punishment 'as a last resort'.

Luckily, nowadays there are few people left who do not understand the great variety of ways in which people (including children!) learn, and the need therefore (*a*) to adapt teaching methods to the pupil and (*b*) to do all that is possible to ensure success. When a teaching method is proving successful all is well—but when individual children do not respond, the teacher needs a variety of other methods which can be tried. The alphabetic method may well be one of these; and 'suit' a particular learner.

Primary Education, H.M.S.O., 1959:

There is something to be learned from each method which has been found useful in the past. Most teachers of young children will agree that just as we recognise objects by the evidence and countercheck of our senses, so children are helped to read by having a variety of aids and methods available to them, reading now by the look of the word, now by its initial sound, now by guessing from the context. . . . For most children a stage will come when some teaching of combinations of sounds, coupled with an explanation of its limitation as a key to reading will increase confidence and a readiness to tackle new words.

Colour cues

Since 1959 other 'methods' have come into being, and they, too, must be looked at for possible approaches. Many solutions to the problem of irregular sound-spelling have been attempted, colour being one. In 1899, The Dale Readers were published using some coloured letters: red for vowels, yellow for silent consonants, blue for unvoiced and black for voiced consonants, plus 'rimes' of warning to draw attention to irregularities or spelling difficulties. In 1962 C. Gattegno produced a reading scheme *Words in Colour* using more than forty colours in an attempt to help children to make the correct sound when translating a printed letter. In 1967 J. K. Jones produced yet another device, combining three colours, red, blue and green with shapes, e.g. circles, squares and rectangles, so that the pages have coloured letters and black letters on coloured shapes. E. and W. Bleasdale's *Reading by Rainbow* also uses colour as a cue, but here it is suggested that the children should only write in black so that there is no 'change-over' problem. While approving this reason it is not so easy to accept the precept offered later. 'Try the black sound first, and if it does not make sense change to the red sound.' This appears to the writer an unfortunate confusion of concepts between colour and sound.

The writer's objection to all such colour cues is that

(*a*) they divert attention from the overall shape of the word and involve considerable numbers of eye movements;

(*b*) they have to be learned and then unlearned and discarded; and

(*c*) there is a high incidence of defective colour vision particularly in boys.

Other schemes have involved the use of diacritical marks, ranging from the fairly generally known māte or măt to quite elaborate signs. Here again, the objections (*a*) and (*b*) given above hold true.

The initial teaching alphabet

The i.t.a. Characters

No	Character	Name	Example	Traditional spelling
1	æ	ae	ræt	rate
2	b	bee	big	big
3	c	kee	cat	cat
4	d	dee	dog	dog
5	ee	ee	seet	seat
6	f	ef	fill	fill
7	g	gae	gun	gun

No	Character	Name	Example	Traditional spelling
8	h	hae	hat	hat
9	i̇e	i̇e	i̇eland̦	island
10	j	jae	ji̇eant	giant
11	k	kae	kit	kit
12	l	el	lamp	lamp
13	m	em	man	man
14	n	en	net	net
15	œ	o	bœt	boat
16	p	pee	pig	pig
17	r	rae	run	run
18	s	ess	sad̦	sad
19	t	tee	tap	tap
20	ue	u	fue	few
21	v	vee	van	van
22	w	wae	will	will
23	y	i-ae	yell	yell
24	z	zed, zee	fizz	fizz
25	ʃ	ʃess	houʃes	houses
26	ᴡh	whae	when	when
27	ᴄh	chae	ᴄhick	chick
28	ᴛh	ith	ᴛhaut	thought
29	ᴛh	thee	ᴛhe	the
30	ʃh	ish	ʃheperd̦	shepherd
31	ʒ	zhee	jud̦ʒ	judge
32	ŋ	ing	siŋ	sing
33	ɑ	ah	fɑr	far
34	au	a	aut	ought
35	a	at	appl	apple
36	e	et	egg	egg
37	i	it	d̦ip	dip
38	o	ot	hot	hot
39	u	ut	ugly	ugly
40	ω	oot	bωk	book
41	ꞷ	oo	mꞷn	moon
42	ou	ow	bou	bough
43	oi	oi	toi	toy

The writer sets great store by the suggestion that there shall be no formal teaching of spelling until the children are reading fairly fluently (this is approximately the point at which phonics would be introduced to children who started on Look and Say). As a result it is expected that the children will write very freely, being unhampered by emphasis on correct spelling.

i.t.a. became a major research project in 1961 under the auspices of the Reading Research Unit of London University Institute of Education, but in 1967 lack of funds brought this to an end. Various bodies made their own comparative evaluations and in 1969 the Schools Council published the findings of Professor Warburton and Vera Southgate. It is obviously difficult to distinguish between the value of the medium as such and the Hawthorne effect of the enthusiasm of its advocates.

The acceptance of i.t.a. has ranged from a whole local education authority (Oldham) in one area to its use in remedial classes or with individual children elsewhere. A number of publishers offer i.t.a. versions of reading schemes as well as books aimed at younger children; and these are available in most public libraries. It seems that teachers are either strongly for or against i.t.a., the expense being a not inconsiderable factor in the argument. In general the Warburton and Southgate evaluation came out in favour of i.t.a., but many people feel that more research into the early stages of reading is called for before unquestioning approval is possible. What is undoubtedly true is that the medium *of itself* is not the answer—good teaching is still required. Sir James claims that i.t.a. is equally suited both to Look and Say and Phonic approaches, and that no change in methods of teaching is required. His opponents maintain that although there seems plenty of evidence that some children learn to read more quickly with i.t.a., the reading ability of children taught in T.O. draws level after a time, and that the transfer to T.O. can give more difficulty than i.t.a. supporters suggest. i.t.a. has been used as a remedial measure with adults as well as children, and has also met with some success in teaching reading overseas, where English is a second language.

So much then for the devices aimed at helping children to decode the written symbols into the sounds that will give meaning to words. There are valuable sources of advice for classroom procedures in the teacher's manuals of graded reading schemes using a Phonic approach, and in those supporting Look and Say followed by Phonics. Some manuals also offer help in the assessment of readiness and practising teachers will doubtless select from all such sources to suit individual children in their care. Many of the games and apparatus described in the previous chapter can be adapted to train auditory discrimination as well as visual discrimination. It is obviously essential that the children develop a sensitive and accurate ear and precise diction and pronunciation.

Auditory discrimination

Lamoureux and Lee, *Learning to Read through Experience*:

> If a child does not hear distinctly he cannot be expected to tie up the correct printed symbol with the correct sound. If he is not in the habit of listening for the lesser differences in sounds of words, if the*m* and the*n* sound no different to him, if he does not distinguish between a*m*, a*n* and a*nd*, he probably will not read them correctly. We must be certain that his hearing is adequate and then we must train him to listen to these small differences in sound.

For these reasons some teachers feel that phonic approaches are less suitable in areas of linguistic deprivation, as first, such children seldom speak accurately, and second, they frequently have not the sustained concentration necessary to listen carefully and mimic small differences in sound, such as that between thi*ng* and thi*nk*. However some teachers find that the use of hand mirrors, or even standing side-by-side, with a teacher, facing a large mirror can awaken interest in correct mouth formation and tongue and lip movements. There is also the problem that the sound of your own voice is so difficult to compare with the sound of other people's voices, as so much of your own voice has passed to your ear through facial bones, e.g. young children believe they are saying 'three' when in fact the sound they make is 'free' or even 'thwee', and will argue hotly that they *did* say it *right*! It sometimes helps to ask children to shut their eyes while listening to a sound. Even quite young children respond to a tape recorder. The teacher says the word or sentence and leaves a gap on the tape for the child to repeat what he has heard. When this is replayed it sometimes makes it possible for the learner both to hear his mistake and correct it. There are numerous other machines available nowadays aimed at producing sound to link with the visual symbol. The Language Master 'speaks' words on flash-cards and has the advantage of the card moving from right to left, thus presenting the word from left to right. The problem with both these is that unless headphones are fitted the sound is a distraction to other children. The ultimate, costing several hundred pounds, is the Talking Typewriter, which 'speaks' the letter sound as it is typed. Many other teaching machines have a contribution to make, such as those self-corrective ones which flash coloured lights to indicate right and wrong answers, which are intended to increase motivation. Most of them are so costly that few schools can afford them and many teachers would feel that they are really only needed in a remedial situation anyway. But an imaginative teacher plus a tape recorder and perhaps a multi-pupil hearing attachment can produce a wealth of phonic teaching material at minimum cost of time and money.

Early stages of phonic training (see chapter 6)

'There's none so deaf as those that won't hear!'

Just as children learned to speak by imitating sounds which had meaning, so the teacher's first job is to contrive situations in which listening is found to be meaningful and worthwhile. The most useful stories, rhymes and songs at this stage are those that involve repetition and participation. On subsequent hearings, the children's alertness and expressive faces bear witness that they are listening with *expectancy*. This is proof of understanding—growing verbal memory and their delight in joining in means that the experience is worthwhile. The converse, of learning *not* to join in, is also valuable—the repetitive rhymes where the words or verses disappear one by one are exercises in self-control as well as listening.

Phonic games

'I spy' games with letter sounds (not names) are always popular—and the mistakes made are a valuable guide as to the children's powers of hearing and comprehension. As skill grows, the sound can be the ending or the middle as well as the initial. If the teacher keeps a check-list she can ensure that she practises a series of letters and digraphs, in ascending order of difficulty. Lists of phonic sounds are given in teacher's manuals, though there is not usually absolute agreement as to sequence. Most children take an interest in their own names and those of their friends and pets, and a little experimenting will help the making of an acceptable check-list.

A tape recording of sounds to guess—asking children to make sounds for their friends to copy or guess; tongue-twisters; riddles, nursery rhymes, Kim's game and flashcards are all of interest to the children. Just as odd-man-out exercises are useful for visual discrimination, so the same odd-man-out puzzles should be prepared for aural discrimination, e.g. 'make bake bat cake' or 'top tip mop pop'. As soon as the children can invent their own puzzles they should be encouraged to do so, and their mistakes noted for future direct teaching sessions. N.B. Matching card games, bingo, completion puzzles, sorting activities can all be made with *sounds* in mind as well as *visual* stimuli.

As soon as the children's powers of concentration allow, individual letters must be learned, first by their sound names and subsequently by their letter names. It is usually best to start with voiced consonants such as b, and to avoid digraphs such as br, bl, etc. If these letters are available as large flashcards they can be used by the children for

guessing games. Initially the teacher places

touching a ball, a book, a basket, etc., and later the children take turns to do the same. This helps to link the sight of the symbol with its sound. As their knowledge of sounds grows the capital form should

be added. At first shown together, ☐ B b

and later separately ☐ B ☐ b

Matching games, both of the symbols, and pairing the sound to the symbol will consolidate this. As many as possible of the words that are found in the first reading book need to be learned at this stage. Wall stories, rhyme sheets, home-made books and charts will build up confidence in the children and words will begin to be recognised out of their original context. Flashcards of relevant words in popular stories will also be useful. Some teachers are skilful at inventing stories so that the children can each hold a word card and stand up and show it when the teacher uses it. At first strong emphasis on the word, or even a look in the direction of the holder, may be necessary. All the usual flashcard games can also be used.

Summary The aim is for the children to understand that a mark on paper (letter and later word) has a particular sound, and that this sound is consistent. Regular sounds and words are therefore used at first.

Middle stages of phonic training

When a vocabulary has been acquired sufficient to read the first book of the series, and a lead into books through home-made wall stories and books has been given, the children's interest in the characters and events must be aroused. This is often done by stories about the characters, some of which lend themselves to dramatisation by the children. The aim is that the first book shall be read with enjoyment and the minimum of error. It is worth a leisurely preparatory period, so that first impressions of 'reading' are conducive to self-confidence and optimism about the next! Many teachers feel that it is worthwhile to read a favourite story so often that the children know it by heart as this builds up confidence and pleasure.

As soon as the first book is part of the children's repertoire further phonic instruction and more detailed analysis of words is possible. At the same time the words needed for Book 2 must be learned. Many teachers keep the necessary phonic instruction and drill entirely separate from reading as an activity; though they refer to such practice when hearing the children read. At this stage the five vowels in their short form are usually taught, and the regular three-letter words which include them. This is also the stage when some phonic writing exercises, such as those from wheels, ladders, masks and twists (see end of this chapter) and other matching games may be relevant.

Scanning and blending

Another advantage of emphasis on initial letters is that it develops the habit of attacking words from left to right. To encourage careful attention to each letter in turn it is helpful to mask the word with a slip of card, and move this slowly enough to permit each letter to be focused in succession. The same technique is used again when digraphs, letter groups and/or syllables are being learned. When the technique of scanning and identifying letters has been achieved the sounds have to be put together to make words—this is called blending, and may involve a single word or group of letters. This skill is found very difficult by some children and the writer believes that this may be due to insufficiently developed visual discrimination, which would suggest postponing the attempt to await maturation, or else using a Look and Say technique instead.

There are two schools of thought as to the best method of blending b a t. One is to treat ba as a sound and add t. The other is to sound the b and add the at. The writer supports the former, as first, it permits an extended sound due to the presence of the vowel, and second, it begins to help the children to take in more of a word than a single letter, i.e. a good eyeful. Phonic apparatus will be made to match the method used—in this case either

At this stage there should be a rapid acquisition of regular three-letter words, which though learned phonically, become, in fact, a sight vocabulary. Depending on the children's varying interests and degree of expertise, word jigsaws, puzzles and other games of matching and building are useful practice, and some direct teaching of spelling is acceptable. Many children are now both able and willing to learn a number of prefixes and suffixes such as wh sh th and ing or tion and some become fascinated by analysing long words such as 'caterpillar' into reliable syllables cat-er-pill-ar, which can be sounded out. On the other hand, rote sounding-out of letters which cannot be blended into meaningful words needs to be avoided. The writer has met many children in remedial classes who are 'stuck' with the habit of attacking every word letter by letter and thus prevented from getting meaning (and hence satisfaction). This can be even more disastrous if letter names are used, e.g. 'it' analysed as eye-tee or 'once' as oh-en-see-ee or even by sound the, teh-heh-eh there, therefore and ăpple or āim, etc.

Final stages of phonic training

These will be closely linked to the teaching of spelling and attention to how to discover which of the alternative sounds is represented by vowels. It is also important to help the children to sort out irregular words which are best learned as wholes and regular groups of letters which can help to unlock meaning. It is important that children are not required to read silently before their powers of visual discrimination are well developed and inner speech makes it possible to *think* sounds. A word that lies in someone's passive vocabulary may need to be vocalised before it is recognised. Recall is only possible with words which are familiar. Intelligent guessing must be applauded—and logical substitutions of words accepted. If children complete the sense by using the 'wrong' word, this means that they are thinking ahead and expecting the text to make sense. The ability to read quickly and intelligently depends a great deal on anticipation; and this needs fostering from the beginning. It is usually easy enough, by judicious questioning, to get the learner to look again and discover the 'right' word from context or slower sounding-out.

Left to right eye movement

In general, the sequence of phonic training should stress the left to right eye movement and accentuate what is dependable rather than what is not. Children love catch words if these are approached light-heartedly and delight in chanting nonsense such as 'The lam*b* and the *g*nat saw a *k*night on an ele*p*-hant!' Some people will consider that the *desire* to spell/read a certain word is a greater motivation than a logical progression from regular to irregular, and from single to double or treble-letter combinations. Sometimes the collecting instinct results in a craze for word lists. One teacher I know started two posters and tables of objects, one for d and one for b. The interest spread throughout the school, and the collection of pictures and articles lined both sides of a long corridor—many of them contributed by parents.

Another child, whose parents were crossword addicts, developed a desire to fill a book with his word collections, while another child brought a map to school and carefully copied out all the names on it matching and sorting them with all kinds of subtlety. (Column graphs and Venn diagrams are useful techniques here.) This interest is reminiscent of modern verse, where words are selected which rhyme at the beginning or in the middle, rather than at the end in the traditional manner.

Apparatus and activities

Some of the better known activities are:

1 Tapping rhythms to match names
  'Jenny, Ann, Benjamin and Christopher'
  or 'Pansy, Rose, Daffodil and Marigold'
2 Pairing articles or names

   (i) initial letters   book, pin, ball, spoon, hat
   (ii) final letters   bat, pin, ball, spoon, hat
   (iii) middle letters   book, pin, ball, spoon, hat

obviously (ii) and (iii) are more advanced

3 Odd-man-out with articles and later pictures and/or names
4 Dominoes with pictures and later names and parts of names
5 Capital and lower case matching
6 Word jigsaws—especially blends
7 Matching

(i) whole words and parts

(ii) words and their plurals, regular cat cats and irregular mouse, mice

8 Wall and individual picture dictionaries

   (i) interest

   (ii) sorted into a relationship

   (iii) alphabetic

   (iv) digraphs

9 Phonic wheels, ladders and masks

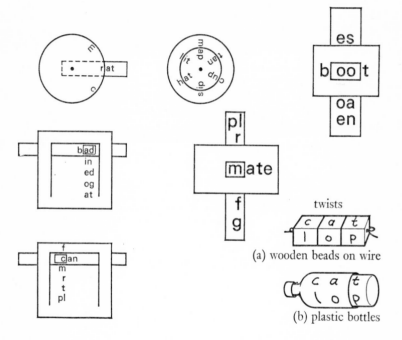

twists

(a) wooden beads on wire

(b) plastic bottles

10 Mapping

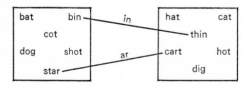

11 *Heads and tails and middles*

    (i) add letters

             a
             at
             bat
             bats or battles, etc.

    (ii) make new words grass   thin

                              grin

    (iii) break up words carrot   carpet
                 car rot   car pet
    (iv) treasure hunt, find and underline ar
         star starling heart stare cart apart

12 Sets (*a*) balloons, ring 'da' set

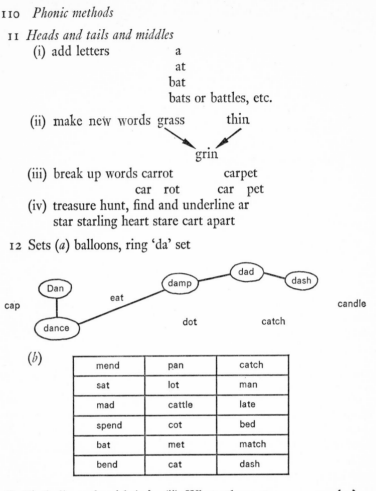

    (*b*)

mend	pan	catch
sat	lot	man
mad	cattle	late
spend	cot	bed
bat	met	match
bend	cat	dash

(i) Find all words with 'at' (ii) What other sets can you make?

    (*c*) *Rhymes* play   hope

           rope   ring

           cart   pond

           thing   stay

           fond   start

    (*d*) Crossing out letters, digraphs on syllables or hectographed
    pages or discarded books

13 *Draw pictures* of things whose names

(*a*) start with:

| c | cr | cl | etc. |

(*b*) end with

| s | sh | rk | etc. |

(*c*) have in the middle a e i o u

| ar | ea | an | etc. |

14 *Families* initial, ending or middles.

bat	church	bat	boot
bird	chop	cat	moon
brown	charm	sat	wood
back	chick	flat	loom
black	chest	chat	door

N.B. arrange to emphasize similarities (see chapter 10).

N.B. distinguish between teaching (self-corrective) activities and testing, which must be checked by the teacher or more advanced child in a family grouping situation perhaps?

The alphabet

Time was when the alphabet was taught as an introduction to reading—and many parents are critical and uneasy if their children are not taught this in their early days at school. It is not unusual for children to come to school being able to recite the alphabet and the digits 1–10 or further. While this is 'good' in that it leads to parental approval it can be 'bad' in that strings-of-sounds, without meaning, can make it more difficult for their parts to be isolated and associated with meaning. We all know how difficult it is to *think* about what we are saying when the words are over familiar. The writer once heard a young teacher embark on the Lord's Prayer when she intended to say grace! We are also most of us aware of the nuisance of 'perseveration', the unwanted verse, quote, a tune which runs in the head against one's will. This makes it difficult to select the item required without having first to work through the previous members of the series, e.g. the need to recite 1 × 7 up to 6 × 7 before being able to give 49 as the answer to 7 × 7.

In many schools nowadays the alphabet is gradually acquired as a useful frame of reference, and the placing of letters taught more often in relation to each other rather than as a string-of-sounds. The use of alphabetic picture dictionaries, word lists, indexes and reference books will lead to a working knowledge of the letters and their sequence—on which the alphabet can be built. As the children grow older they will learn to use dictionaries and other reference books and this would seem a better sequence than the learning by heart (rote) of the alphabet before understanding of its significance is possible (see chapter 10 for spelling games).

9 Writing

True ease in writing comes from art not chance
As those move easiest who have learned to dance.
Blest be the gracious power who taught mankind
To stamp a lasting image on the mind.
Beasts may convey, and tuneful birds may sing
Their mutual warblings in the opening spring.
'Tis to the Pen and Press we mortals owe
All we believe and almost all we know.

From *Essay on Criticism* by Alexander Pope (1688–1744):
(used as a school copybook exercise, nineteenth century)

The distinction between handwriting and content

The lines above do not draw the distinction between the skill of writing, graphic control and the content of writing, which depends upon the ability to select words. The former is a technique, whereas the latter is an attempt at communication. There is little argument as to whether writing (or print) is legible but infinite disagreement as to the ability of a writer to put over his meaning; to write artistically; to compose a successful advertisement and so on. On the other hand, legibility can come under discussion in specialised circumstances such as the design of road signs (to be read at speed and in different weather conditions), lettering to be carved on monuments or public buildings, trademarks, neon lighting or lettering (by which I intend to include figures) which is intended to have symbolic association. For example, I have seen a van selling fish and chips, where drawings of small fish formed the first word and the second was composed of fried potato sticks! The ampersand presumably does not represent salt or vinegar?

In earlier times so few people were able to write that scribes were held in esteem—employed only by the rich and mighty—and even today there are cultures where the public letter writer is needed. Religious orders early discovered the extra respect that reading and writing inspired in ordinary people—and for centuries reading, writing, and in some cases, mathematics were chiefly the province of the priests. In the middle ages most monasteries produced books, and although the scribes were extraordinarily skilful graphically, some mistakes made proved that many of them could not read what they wrote. This has an amusing parallel in the eighteenth century, when the wealthy had porcelain table-ware made in France which was shipped to the East for decoration. On one occasion, a French designer being short of a colour drew an arrow to that piece of the crest with the legend, 'This should be red'. In due course the entire service was returned to France with every crest bearing its arrow and these words! Nowadays we expect writers to be able to read the words they write, but we do not always recognise what a highly sophisticated and complex skill handwriting is.

A skill has to be taught—and hence learned. Efficient and economical learning requires motivation and there is this 'stage of readiness' which enables learning to take place without undue stress. Teachers have to learn to recognise and assess such readiness in each individual, and, as with readiness for reading, a passive awaiting is not enough. There is no doubt that learning to read or write is very much more difficult if the two techniques are considered entirely separately. The problem is that in order to write and spell, individual letters have to be identified and shaped in a set sequence, left to right, whereas in expert reading, individual letters will scarcely ever be concentrated on. All manner of visual stimuli serve as cues to the reader but speedy silent and expressive oral reading are not possible if every letter has to be focused, digraphs noted and sounds blended.

Desire to write

As in reading, the most potent motivation is the *desire* to write, and this is closely allied with the understanding of the usefulness of being able to write and the value of the written symbols, words and figures. This is frequently demonstrated to the adult by imitative play—the children offering scribbles which they describe as letters, invitations, books, etc. Just as children 'read' to their toys and peers, so they usually 'write' and teach their toys and friends to write. A great deal of personal pride is early involved in these achievements. My daughter, at the age of three and a half, was most indignant when her father showed an interest in her older brother's sums and said, 'I'm doing sums too—I'm counting spots'. She was drawing round a penny and colouring these spots, and writing squiggles beneath them as the figures she 'counted', quite unaware that her squiggles had any less significance than her brother's digits.

Scribbling

Very many children work their way through a similar sequence of scribbling (see diagram) which is probably dependent on the sequence

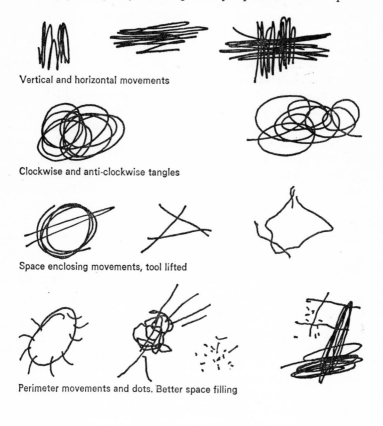

Vertical and horizontal movements

Clockwise and anti-clockwise tangles

Space enclosing movements, tool lifted

Perimeter movements and dots. Better space filling

Later, travelling

Typical sequences of scribbling

of brain maturation. This is well described by Grözinger, *Scribbling, Writing and Painting*, unfortunately now out of print. Less well known is the value to children of using both hands at once. Many more teachers nowadays offer writing materials to both hands, and the children who use both hands often tackle their drawing with great vigour and enjoyment. It is not generally known that the medieval craft guilds required their members to be ambidextrous. Apprentices were compelled to use tools in alternate hands on successive days. Once you know this it is easier to understand the perfection of carving in the less accessible nooks and crannies of ancient buildings. Another safeguard of high standards were the heavy penalties laid upon those discovered working by artificial light. We will return to this a little later when we look at handedness.

Readiness is also dependent, naturally, on physical development. Pen or pencil grip depends on fine muscle control and is not developed early. Good handwriting is also influenced by posture which does not strain the eyes or lead to unnecessary fatigue. Other physical aspects which require assessment are the perfection or otherwise of the eye structure; the degree of visual discrimination acquired; any other bodily handicaps or defects; the chronological age of the pupil and the extent of his intellectual development. His emotional development will influence his powers of attention and concentration and the confidence he displays in attacking unknown situations and meeting success and failure. Lastly, his general language level such as vocabulary (passive and active), powers of speech and delight in words are all of significance.

Drawing and painting

Motivation to write will obviously grow naturally out of the child's pleasure in drawing and painting, but also will be dependent upon the availability of the necessary materials and the experience of seeing other people write, and understanding *why* they do so. There will be the normal desire to do something himself—copying, in fact. If such attempts meet with approval (i.e. success) they immediately acquire meaning and become pleasurable and will be repeated. As time goes on, reinforcement in the shape of more understanding of usefulness; the relation of writing to other activities such as reading; the example of parents, teachers, older siblings and peers; being read to and seeing books consulted for help and information; the desire to communicate and to share discoveries will all increase this motivation. A well-prepared classroom environment or home stimulation such as nature tables, or colour displays, etc., for instance room labels, names on pegs and possessions, wall stories, picture captions and the respect paid to his own paintings will all increase his interest. The moment when he *really* understands that sounds can be made to appear on paper (and the converse—that marks on paper represent sounds and hence meaning) is a landmark and dramatic forward surges of progress can result. Dr Maria Montessori called it 'an explosion into writing'.

As children progress they become aware that very small differences in shape have major importance, e.g. that ϵ is not the same as ɘ. This must be very difficult to comprehend when one considers how often in life the position of a shape in space is without significance. Decorated plates on a table are accepted as equally useful no matter which way the pattern faces; or an earlier experience is of learning to recognise mother's face when she leans over your pram from any direction. We have all seen children enjoying surveying the world from between their legs—or hanging upside down or standing on their heads. The distortion in size of adult heads from the lying, crawling and early walking positions must be great. I once saw a book illustrated entirely from the dog's eye view and was shocked into realising that this is the young child's elevation too, seeing the underside of tables rather than the top for instance or huge feet and legs and diminutive heads and hats. No wonder there is such delight and astonishment in trying on parents' clothes or attempting to get inside a doll's house!

Analysis of letter shapes

In order to write, children have to learn to form letters. An analysis of the letter formation of print letters and digits shows that certain pencil movements have to be made much more often than others.

anti-clockwise	↺	*a c d e f g i o q u w y*	and	**6 9 0**
clockwise	↻	*b h j m n p r*	and	**2 3 5**
vertical/horizontal	↓ →	k l t K H T	and	**1 4 7**
chevron ∧∧∨		v w x y z A W		
s	S	and 8		

t is odd man out in relative proportion they

they

A natural route into letter-making is via patterns. Marion Richardson was a pioneer in this field. All young children enjoy rhythms and repeats. Even adults find it hard to resist trailing a stick along fence rails or to avoid altering their pace to match paving stones or the sound of a band. If children are offered colours to use and a variety of different media, the early stages of hand control need not be drudgery.

Materials to encourage hand-eye co-ordination

A rich variety of materials will stimulate sensitive and delicate hand movements and hence help to develop hand-eye co-ordination. To list them quickly:

Finger paint, slip (liquid clay), paint, coloured inks
Fingers, feathers, sticks, brushes, sponges
Chalks, crayons, felt pens, pencils, pens
Wet sand, dry sand, water, soapsuds
Clay, 'Plasticine', dough, paste, plaster
Chalk boards, paper, slate, glass, fablon, trays
Tracing paper, texture surfaces, wax and heelball
Pattern and picture cards, tracing copies
Pipe cleaners, wire, plastic covered flex and rope, hairpins
String, carpet wool, rope, matchsticks, mosaic bricks
Sandpaper letters, stencils, cut-outs, mirrors
and probably many more besides.

Natural surfaces invite marking, scratching and incising—misted window panes and mirrors (to say nothing of dirty cars!) appear irresistible—and when moisture is not available, spittle does splendidly! Young children will spend hours painting outside with water and can be led into discussions as to the 'magic' of evaporation. Marbling (the floating of oil-based colour on water) and the taking-off of the design by gently laying paper on the surface of the water, can increase the delicacy and control of children's hands. But in due course nothing will satisfy but 'real' grown-up writing.

Teacher's assessment of readiness

The teacher's everlasting responsibility to her pupils is to contrive success for them and thus build up their confidence in themselves and the worthwhileness of effort. This is sometimes done by exactly meeting their level of attainment—but more usually by starting with something known to be within their powers—and by encouragement and preserving a warm, permissive atmosphere in the room, where failure is met with sympathy and a confident 'Never mind, you'll soon get it right!' The children will raise their own aims and compete against themselves. Careful observations (and records of the same!) of the children's movement and powers of balance and co-ordination when playing freely—working with small and big apparatus in P.E., and handling knives, forks, scissors, clothing fastenings, etc., will all help the teacher to gauge the degree of readiness for small writing tools such as pencils. A great deal of pleasure can be gained by children still holding brushes and giant chalks in a fist or palmar grip. For these children large areas of wall faced with matt but unstainable paint and chalkboard are essential, so that large movements are possible. It is sometimes necessary to help parents to recognise that 'More haste, less speed' can not only lead to anxiety and tension but may de-motivate their children so that they avoid writing situations for a very long time. It is always more difficult to re-build confidence than to use natural desires and extend natural stages of growth. A slower start can often mean accelerated progress later. Signs of strain like breath-holding; tight neck muscles; eye rubbing; fidgeting and irritability are warnings that the conditions or activity are over-demanding.

Motivation and fatigue

Strain must be avoided physically, intellectually and emotionally. If children are sitting to write, the relationship of chair to writing surface must be considered. A lower seat level fits a sloped surface but a higher seat is necessary for a flat surface. The chair must be matched to leg length also—and it is quite unrealistic to offer only one height of chair and table in any one classroom. Many children are happier kneeling or standing to write at first—and some do splendidly squatting; the weight of bone in their pelvic girdles making this a naturally comfortable position. The writing surface must be steady also. Bulldog clips to hold paper to pieces of hardboard may make all the difference.

Intellectual fatigue is much harder to judge and is closely linked with emotional fatigue. Forced labour results from imposed tasks, irrelevant to the children's purposes, outside their understanding, over-prolonged or demanded when their interest lies elsewhere. The reason for writing must be clear to the children, and preferably derive from their chosen work of the moment. Children quickly see the reason for writing a list of food that the hamster may eat, so that it does not have a tummy ache! They may well be less interested in writing 'Today is Monday. It is cloudy' or even 'Mary saw a red 'bus'. The teacher will be alert to the need to illustrate the usefulness of writing. She will say things like: 'I'll just write that down, then I'll remember to buy some tiny buttons for you.' 'Please take this note to the kitchen and cook will lend us some currants.' 'Here's a letter for Mummy to ask if you may come to the zoo.' 'This piece of card has the recipe for peppermint creams written on it.' 'That is your painting: I know because I wrote your name on it.' Parents can also help at home by calling attention to shopping lists, letters of thanks, labels, tickets, invitations and so on.

Techniques in teaching handwriting

The need to write stems from the need to record; to share; to make things; and children take time to realise that the ability to read and write means that you can cross the barriers of time and space. It will help at first if the number of alternative shapes are kept to the minimum. The style of script in writing should be identical wherever possible with the type the children will meet elsewhere in school. Fortunately many books for young children now use a and g rather than a and g. Teachers have realised for a long time that an ounce of example is worth a pound of exhortation—and take pride in high standards of display and lettering. Examples that are offered for tracing and copying are carefully written so that shape and scale suit the child's tool. Parents can help here by finding out the shape of letter and figure the school prefers and then remembering to use it too, so that children are not confused by different symbols such as 4 and 4, 3 and 3, 7 and 7, *ℬ* and B, BARBARA, Barbara and *Barbara*. Another common area of confusion is the too-early teaching of spacing and punctuation. In some schools lined paper is used in an attempt to hasten regularity of line, and even rules like 'tall letters must touch both lines'. The result is all too often deplorable as regards proportion, e.g.

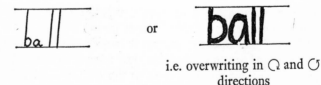

i.e. overwriting in ↻ and ↺
directions

I have seen schools where children were required to leave a finger's width between each word! Surely what we are aiming for is a relaxed, legible, well-proportioned hand, with placing on the page suited to the size of letter that feels natural? Adults can change the size of their writing to suit the occasion, and know how to choose the tool for the job—Witch pen for church sale poster, broad nib for large sheet of paper, fine ball pen or hard lead for a plan or a tracing. But this was not learned in the first few months of learning to write. When children understand the *need* for spacing words, i.e. ease of reading, they learn to place words quickly, but this need is only recognised when words are thought of in a phrase or sentence, and the hand is keeping up more easily with thought.

Another responsibility for a teacher is to set realistic standards. If an adult is drafting an important letter—say, of condolence or application for a job—he is unusual if he starts straight away on the fair copy. Most of us make a draft, revise and correct it, or even ask a friend for advice—and only when all the planning is complete start on the technical stage of writing it on paper. It is surely most unreasonable to demand that children are creative and inventive and simultaneously can pay attention to 'best' writing, correct spelling, punctuation, layout and choose the best tool and paper at the same time? During a scribing and copying session this may be possible, but insistence too soon only results in a check on self-expression and a meagre choice of words, i.e. those he is certain he *can* spell. Anxiety will lead to tension and a lowering of standards.

Copying from the blackboard or wall is tiring. If white chalk is used on a black board and the children are writing in pencil or ink— the visual image is a positive/negative one. In any case the exercise demands constant re-focusing. If the children have decided to practise a phrase perhaps 'With best wishes for Christmas' it is better to have the copy written on a slip of card which can be placed on the paper the child is using, and moved down each time to cover the previous effort. In this way the model is copied each time, not the child's own writing and no visual memory is required. When us- ing a copy book, it is sensible to write the first effort on the bottom line, the second on the one above and so on. This again focuses attention on the model—not the child's own effort. Needless to say, exhortations such as 'Be quick!' 'Be more careful!' seldom result in much improvement as they divert attention from the job in hand and can lead to muscle tension.

With experience it is easy to judge from children's drawings and writings whether the child was at ease when working on them. Sign of tension are displayed by pressure on the paper, the evenness of a repeated letter in shape and pressure, line-flow, deterioration, letters written over several times and so on. Other obvious reasons for fatigue are poor lighting, lack of ventilation, being crowded, placing a left-handed child against a right-handed and not at the corner of a table where his arm will be unrestricted, using the wrong tool (surface and writing agent) or being kept writing for too long at a time.

Stages in learning to write

For many children the stages in writing are as follows:

(*a*) random spontaneous movements;

(*b*) noticing that a mark results;

(*c*) deliberate repetition, i.e. testing if it happens again;

(*d*) repetition, i.e. practice;

(*e*) intentional movement;

(*f*) additional possibilities discovered with different tools and colours;

(*g*) marks designed to make a definite shape—perhaps lines or dots;

(*h*) scribbling;

(*i*) controlled and repetitive scribbling;

(*j*) sometimes at this point the scribble is named, e.g. 'Letter to Father Christmas';

(*k*) scribbling with intention and imitation—probably 'travelling';

(*l*) understanding of communication through writing;

(*m*) desire to write 'properly';

(*n*) ability to trace;

(*o*) ability to copy;

(*p*) independent letter formation;

(*q*) ability to assess accuracy and to know if it is 'right' or 'wrong', i.e. matching;

(*r*) growth of self-criticism;

(*s*) willingness to learn different letter forms;

(*t*) ability to select standard of performance, i.e. casual or 'best' writing.

N.B. (*k*) to (*p*) are the periods where suitable materials must be available and the child must possess enough emotional stability to be willing to persevere. This is the most hazardous period—when pressure from home or school can quickly result in regression and a desire to avoid such writing situations for fear of failure.

N.B. writing (historically anyhow) preceded reading.

Man's sequence in learning to write in symbols

Space does not permit a review of the historical development of scripts, and reference has already been made in chapter 3 to the problem of interpreting symbols; and the sequence of children's symbolic drawings of the human figure. However, it can easily be seen that letters have developed from representational signs—and we are blessed in that we have a phonic method of recording as opposed to a pictorial one such as the Chinese language, where each character has derived from a pictogram. Some patterns can be found incised or drawn all over the world and controversy waxes strong among archaeologists as to their significance; amusement, religious or from the very beginning an attempt to transmit thought? We are all familiar with the Dauphin's present to Henry V of tennis balls—a calculated insult—but we may not know of the Scythians who sent King Darius a bird, a mouse, a frog and five arrows. He had no doubt as to their meaning, which was 'Persians, can you fly like a bird, hide yourself in the ground like a mouse, leap through the grass like a frog? If you cannot, do not go to war with us. We shall overwhelm you with arrows.' Children enjoy stories like this and soon see that writing is an easier and more precise form of message.

Man has used tallies or knotted string as mnemonics; picture stories (the modern strip cartoon shows no sign of dying) and analytic writing developed in the cuneiform of the East and the hieroglyphics of China. Phonetic writing was a great advance—in its most sophisticated form, to date, as the alphabet—and cursive writing increased the possible speed as lower case letters were developed. We have now invented typewriters and shorthand and are back to the position where we have to have modern scribes—our shorthand-typists. Braille is another form of shorthand—this time tactile rather than visual—while morse code can be transmitted with visual and audible symbols. Recording has, then, moved from the representational through to the abstract.

The sequence of bodily development is roughly from the head down and from the centre of the body outwards. The control of gross muscular movements makes it possible for fine muscle movements to be developed. The development of the electric-encephalograph and research into the development of the human brain has resulted in our greatly increased understanding of how the brain functions. One of the aims of education surely is the transformation of the human brain into the human mind? The more a part of the body is used for exploring its environment the larger is the cortical area (see Homunculus diagram, chapter 6, p. 69). This diagram is a vivid illustration of the relative importance of different parts of the body in learning.

Handedness

One characteristic of human beings has always caused great interest, i.e. handedness. The majority of us are right-handed and, in general, society has planned the environment to suit the right-handed. Codes of good manners have usually derived from necessity. The man offered his left arm to a lady to leave his sword arm free with which to defend her. Later he walked on the outside of the pavement to protect her from mud splashes and so on. The left-handed handshake of boy scouts and girl guides was used because it is unusual—the handshake itself is the descendant of the arm clasping which proved your friendship because you were unarmed. In some cultures, left-handedness was believed to be ungodly or the influence of the devil. Perhaps this was not the reason—but not long since children were compelled to write with their right hands. Obviously, if you are to write left to right it is easier to avoid smudging if you use your right hand. The connection of preferred hand and brain formation was not then understood. However some of the medical profession are now seeking to help brain development by 'patterning', i.e. moving a non-developing child's body into the posture that a normal crawling or creeping baby uses—and some encouraging progress has been noted. Such doctors claim that the use of two hands helps to form a well-balanced brain rather than one with a strongly dominant side; and hence strong-handedness. Obviously if a strong preference exists it is foolish to compel a child to use his less skilful hand and the resulting tension and frustration could well lead to such emotional disturbance that faulty speech development could be a symptom of distress.

All manipulative activity helps to develop fine muscle control and co-ordination, but the clumsy, as yet unco-ordinated pupil may need considerable practice with gross motor movement, and, until this is given, be *unable* to improve. It is tempting not to allow such children to give out milk, paint or small tools, for fear of spills—but this is robbing them of the means of learning how *not* to spill. When a spill occurs, sympathy is the order of the day—followed by more practice! Early on in their school life, the teacher will provide opportunities for children to use both hands at once. By comparing patterns, she can quickly discover the preferred hand. Try this experiment yourself. Hold two ball pens or pencils, one in each hand. Breathe out. As you breathe in, start making similar shapes with each hand. By comparing the two sides it will be obvious which hand is the stronger and better controlled, e.g.

Sequences in pattern making

From outside to centre

Clockwise sequence

From outside to centre

Anti-clockwise

Clockwise and anti-clockwise combined

Writing patterns (see diagram for a sequence in pattern making)

When giving children tracing exercises it is, of course, vital that the correct sequence is made. When drawing o, for instance the starting point is at one o'clock and the movement anti-clockwise. This will allow cursive writing to follow without re-learning. Similarly a g must be made with the loop, anti-clockwise, first and the tail second. Many children derive much help first by saying a shape and then by writing it with shut eyes. Take for example the adg progression: a will be written with this verbal accompaniment 'round up down';

with a slight up and down inflection of the voice—and a steady even rhythm.

d will follow with the identical 'round'—but a greatly emphasised and slowed 'up' and a pretty neutral 'down', while g will be written to a verbal accompaniment of 'round' and 'up' as in ɑ but a strong 'down' while the tail is written.

Similar sequences for r n m and h are obvious.

It is unwise to teach capitals and lower case letters together, unless they share line sequence. S s or B b are quite reasonable—but D d is just the reverse. D B is a better pair. Some teachers find that children can be motivated by stories that can be illustrated by letter shapes, e.g.

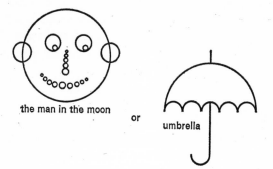

the man in the moon

or

umbrella

the humps ⌒⌒⌒⌒ providing practice for the letter m.

Children love to invent patterns which help in letter formation (see diagram).

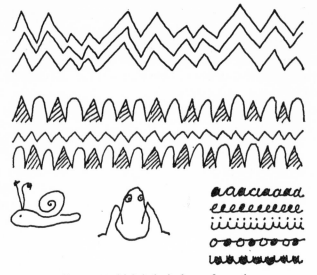

Patterns which help in letter formation

Obviously wall displays of children's writing for competitive reasons is highly undesirable being blatantly unfair. We do not ask children in callipers to run races against those with unimpaired leg muscles and bones! Co-ordination is largely a matter of the development of the nervous system and consequently mostly beyond conscious control. Opportunity for exercise makes it possible for co-ordination to develop—and equally, fear of failure may result in children avoiding such opportunities. However, one way of recording progress has worked in my experience. A book of examples is built up by joining subsequent sheets of paper on top of the preceding ones, in the manner of a wall calendar. Every so often a child makes a drawing or a writing pattern, or later, a few lines of writing. As time goes on, the children become self-critical and do not add a sheet unless they are sure it shows progress. By looking underneath they can see their own progress, and equally the parent and teacher can enjoy the improvement. This is the best form of competition—against one's own efforts. Enough effort and care will result in improvement but too much can have the opposite effect—anxiety, tension and repression.

Dyslexia and dysgraphia

There are two handicaps, dyslexia and dysgraphia, which some children have to overcome. Dyslexia has many definitions but the disability results in the sufferer being unable to make sense of the visual stimuli of words; some people call it word-blindness. This is a most frustrating experience for the child concerned, as, no matter how hard he tries, the ability to make sense of the marks that he can see eludes him. In some cases the eyes move in opposite directions so that a word like Stephen is 'seen' as 'petShen' or 'nehStep'.

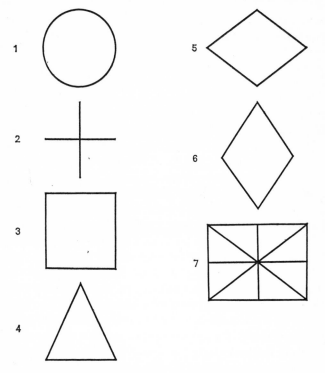

Norman Sims, Educational Psychologist, Bristol L.E.A.: 'The ability to copy these shapes is often a guide to the degree of manual control a child has developed and his perceptual development, e.g. pre-school children will rarely be able to draw more than the first three'

Similarly when writing commences ε is written for 3 or sometimes d for p or b: one severe dyslexic used to write simultaneously with both hands—the right hand making correct shapes from left to right while the left hand made mirror letters from right to left. If he had lived in ancient Greece, he would have been top of the class, as this is how they wrote—a style known as boustrophedon.

THIS IS WRITTEN BOUS
TROPHEDON AND IS NO
T EASY FOR MOST PEOPL
E TO READ AT SIGHT

Dysgraphia is similarly incapacitating—the child being unable to make lines and shapes he wishes. It is difficult for a teacher to decide quickly whether mistakes made by children are the normal ones which time and practice will cure. Needless to say, children who are only slightly dyslexic or dysgraphic will usually overcome this handicap with time and encouragement. Severe dyslexia and dysgraphia needs expert diagnosis and remedial teaching. Most important of all, all adults connected with the sufferer must recognise his *inability* to do better and far from punishing him for his mistakes make special efforts to keep his courage up. It is obviously humiliating and most depressing to watch one's friends forge ahead and be unaware how to do what they can do. The most severely dyslexic child I ever knew read practically overnight—at about ten years—and was unable to explain how he could now translate into sound words and letters that he 'saw' no better than the previous day. This suggests that brain maturation is responsible. What teachers and parents then need to keep in mind is that such a child has been deprived of years of practice and success and that this deprivation will not be compensated for quickly, if ever. Spelling and handwriting will be a real problem—and slow reading must be expected for a very long time. Hence the problem of examinations *in particular* and the amount of reading and writing expected in school and daily life *in general*.

Motivation towards creative writing

Writing, as content, is largely outside the scope of this book. Obviously the interest the teacher and parent shows in the drawings and paintings of a child will help him in his thinking—and more thought will be evident in his illustrations. Usually he will enjoy seeing his teacher or mother write words at his dictation beneath or even on his picture. Fairly soon he likes to trace over such letters, often in colour, or later, write the sentence again, beneath the adult's lettering. As time goes on, he becomes independent and adds his own words or text to his pictures. Eventually his ability to communicate in words exceeds his ability to communicate in pictures and he writes stories rather than draws them. If he has experienced a rich language environment—enjoyed fantasy, folk tales, poetry, riddles and jokes—being trained in having the hearing ear and the seeing eye as well as sensitive hands, his need to share his pleasure results in creating with words, and in his turn he will write stories and poems—fantasy, fiction and factual. From time to time he will embellish these with decorative borders and book covers, illustrations, and maybe arrange his words in patterns or use coloured inks to draw attention to word forms and moods.

If his home and school fosters his social development by drawing attention to the needs and comfort of other people, to issue invitations and letters of thanks; to help him to imagine what it feels like to be smaller and more helpless than he is, or older and more independent, or very old and need care and consideration, then he will write from his own experience, the resulting feelings and with human love and insight.

This account from an Australian magazine, the *Victorian Baptist Witness*, of an eight-year-old Canadian boy's idea of his grandmother is an excellent illustration of the foregoing:

A grandmother is a lady who has no children of her own, so she likes other people's boys and girls. Grandmas don't have anything to do except be there. If they take us for a walk they slow down past pretty leaves and caterpillars.

They never say 'Hurry up'. Usually they are fat, but not too fat to tie our shoes.

They wear glasses and sometimes they can take their teeth out. They can answer questions like why dogs hate cats and why God isn't married.

When they read to us they don't skip words or mind if it's the same story again.

Everyone should try to have a grandma, especially if you don't have television, because grandmas are the only grown-ups who always have time.

This may make us smile—but it should also give us food for thought. What children need most of the adults who care for them is their time, their company and their delight in the children's discoveries.

10 Spelling

W. B. Yeats: 'We should not make light of the troubles of children. They are worse than ours, because we can see the end of our troubles and they can never see any end.'

In the last chapter, reference was made to dyslexia and dysgraphia and it is obvious that children suffering from either of these conditions will be unable to spell accurately. However there are many people who have no such disability yet are very poor spellers. In fact some take an odd pride in this achievement!

Translating speech sounds into visual symbols

In order to spell we have to understand that speech sounds can be identified and transformed into visible marks, and later that we ourselves can make such marks appear at will. For some children, auditory and visual stimuli are quite sufficient—they readily learn to attach sounds to shapes and to string such shapes into word patterns that represent the required sounds—either individual letters or digraphs such as ph or st. For many others, tactile perception is also needed. In the last chapter, mention was made that writing with shut eyes helps some people to do it better—similarly spelling with shut eyes can help some children to 'get it right'. It appears likely that this is closely connected with mental imagery. Those of us who have vivid visual images can 'see' with our mind's eye, and 'read' a word letter-by-letter, thus writing it. Other people can use their visual discrimination in a different way—using recognition, rather than recall memory. These will write two (or more?) versions of the word and recognise the correct one—it 'looks' right, e.g. gauge or guage? or its associate, language or langauge?

This method of spelling depends almost entirely on the experience of having read for long enough to have encountered the correct spelling on many occasions, and on the mental ability to match and sort correctly when presented with two alternatives.

Other people use similar sorting devices, either saying the sequence of letters in inner speech, a whisper or fully voiced to test if it 'hears right', or shutting their eyes to see if the movements they make 'feel right'. There are fewer people who use auditory or kinaesthetic imaging alone as an aid to spelling. Most of us work with a combination of all three—or use one device rather than another for tricky words. It follows that children should be offered as much variety as possible in sensory stimuli so that later they can select the way in which they can best learn to spell—and that their sense organs are developed to be as delicately receptive and discriminating as possible.

Finger painting, wet and dry sand trays, plasticine and clay snake letters, shapes made by unthreaded sewing machines on stiff paper or fine card; cut-outs and stencils; montage and collage; pipe cleaners and wire; every sort of writing tool and even typewriters can all help.

Helen Keller learned geometry with diagrams made from wire—and St Dunstan's trained a patient as a guide by making a wire model of a castle. In his case his hands had been destroyed and he learned the diagram by tracing it with an arm stump. These successes should encourage us in trying to help every child, and to lend support to the modern practice of keeping children with handicaps in ordinary schools rather than segregating them in special ones. The writer has had some experience of designing small adaptations of equipment so that thalidomide and spastic children can be educated alongside so-called normal children. Ingenuity in substituting a different movement for the same action has its counterpart in all problems connected with reading and writing. For example, a thalidomide boy, with flipper hands rather than normal arms, learned to write with a pencil set into a holder about as long as a ruler—and to type both by using his own hands or a stick with a rubber ferrule. The school doors were fitted with a duplicate handle lower down, and he was then able to move more freely about the school as the other children did. The writer feels that children needing remedial teaching in areas such as reading, writing and spelling could often be helped if we tried to approach their problems without prejudice or reliance on traditional methods.

The multi-stimuli approach

A combination of visual perception to see letters, auditory perception to hear them (N.B. inner speech) and tactile perception to write them and accurate visual, auditory and kinaesthetic memory (recognition and recall) are all needed in order to spell. Ease in the technique of writing is also essential. As long as the children have to *think* a letter shape and then reproduce their *thinked* shape they can have little extra attention to give to letter sequence, let alone proportion and eye level.

Alignment and sequence

Many parents and teachers are unduly disturbed by ᵃdᵍh or god for dog. The line level comes with practice, and some comparison between model words such as 'play' and the way the child has written 'plₐy' 'Is it the same? How is it different? Trace mine—Now write yours again. Good!' Alignment is almost entirely dependent on the starting point of a letter and relative proportion takes time to develop. Writing practice as suggested in the previous chapter helps greatly—e.g. ɑdg. The 'god' substitution for 'dog' is usually merely the writing from right to left instead of from left to right. If children are trained to start from the left-hand margin of a page the sequence is controlled by there being no paper to the left!

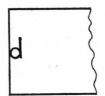

and subsequent letters of necessity follow to the right. Once again, matching mistakes to correct versions is helpful—especially when there is no trace of censure or irritation in the adult voice! The reason for correct spelling should be given 'I won't know what you mean unless you write it this way' but equally we must be always on guard not to lay overmuch stress on accurate spelling, so that children are inhibited and respond either by confining their words to those they know they can spell—or evading a writing situation. In the writer's view, formal teaching of spelling should not begin until children are reading and writing fairly fluently.

Although it is known that we do not read fluently in a letter-by-letter sequence of actions, yet we must spell in this way from left to right. Roughly speaking, about 80 per cent of people are more receptive to visual than to auditory cues; it is therefore efficient to postpone the formal teaching of spelling until such time as the children have had considerable exposure to correct spelling patterns. Tests have shown that by the age of seven or eight years, few children have any perceptual difficulties with inversions and reversals such as d for b so that the later we demand absolute accuracy, i.e. spelling and shape reproduction, the less likely such errors will be made. Also the skill of handwriting is likely to have developed further after all the fine muscle development due to construction, painting and drawing activities and the growing delicacy of manual control that results. Similarly hand–eye co-ordination should be better developed by then.

A parallel is the sequence of touch-typing—individual letters are typed, followed by groups of letters which occur frequently in English spelling—during which time brain pathways are established. Eventually only long, unfamiliar or unconventionally spelled words are typed letter-by-letter. Mistakes are usually homonyms, wrongly translated from shorthand. The sequence of matching and sorting, by which similarities are noted before differences, suggests that we should teach in this way when trying to build confident and accurate spellers. Homonyms should be separated—not taught in pairs. We shall return to this later.

As well as letter sequence per word, there is a complex word sequence per sentence which we *expect* to hear/read (see chapter 6). We all know how tempting it is to supply a word when a speaker hesitates—or even to anticipate the word when we turn a leaf. The experienced reader is more likely to make easy use of these regular patterns of sentence structure and consequently to have more attention to spare for spelling, i.e. letter sequence. Platitudes are hard to escape for this reason. Just as key words in sentences convey essential information and many words are 'fillers-in' (note the telegraphic speech of the eighteen-month-old) so key letters in words can be pointers or focal points around which other letters are grouped. When teaching spelling, these letters should be pointed out and the children helped to see their significance. Some of these letters have phonic significance others have visual (see chapters 7 and 8), hence the teaching techniques must be different for regular and irregular words, and those that can best be learned visually or by auditory methods. A visual key letter is o in 'moon'—you need two in the middle to make the pattern—while ch is a phonic cue in 'church'— you need two, but not in the middle. Children can be helped to treasure hunt the letter o—and note its position in moon, cotton, position, polo, etc.

Nonsense words

If letters had invariant sounds, spelling would be much easier. Read these words aloud to a friend and see if he can spell them:

dink lods besks brelp blasps and glurck
Shut the book and see if you can write them yourself.
How well can you say these?
nkid dsol skseb ipebr spsable ckurgl

What this all adds up to is that spelling is best taught in spelling patterns rather than letter-by-letter, and both tested and practised in *written* form rather than by the saying of letter sequence. The occasions on which we need to dictate spelling are very few compared with the need to write spellings. Spelling bees may be fun—for *some* children—but are pretty unproductive, and for those children who spell almost entirely by sight quite bewildering. In writing, phonemes must be turned into graphemes and, as soon as possible, the thought process turned into visible symbols with as little thought and energy as possible expended on the latter process.

Transfer—the ability to generalise experience—depends on increasing skill in recognising and later recalling the regularities and irregularities of a spoken and printed cluster of sounds and their equivalent in letters. This skill is, of course, matching, sorting and grading once again.

Short- and long-term memory

There are many types of memory, the major divisions being short and long term, recognition and recall. Short-term memory is typified by the ability to look up a strange telephone number and hold the figure sequence long enough for the necessary dialling process. Long-term memory is self-explanatory. Recognition is the ability to recognise the address you require from a column of addresses in the telephone book. Recall is the ability to give the address 'from memory'.

Caught and taught spelling

The writer believes that spelling is *caught* incidentally in the first stages of learning to write—but must be *taught* systematically to most children later on. The best moment is probably the time of phonic instruction. However, we should note that some children appear to need little, if any, instruction in spelling or phonics. It is obviously irrelevant and wearying to such children if they are included in such periods of direct teaching. It is possible that such children read early, have strong visual memory, good co-ordination and pronounced interest in words, leading to early success and hence quick reinforcement. This is the opposite of the vicious circle, but it is hard to analyse or even identify the causes that lead to such desirable effects. Certain it is that some children who are equally keen to acquire the same facility are totally unable to do so.

Teachers need to be able to assess their pupils' performance so as to be economical in their teaching. Most children, at some time, need their attention drawn to the visual and phonic cues by which accurate spelling can be achieved. Spelling rules are one of these cues—but some have so many exceptions that they are not worth the study. What must at all costs be avoided is 'the ferocious correction of spelling' referred to in the Newsom Report. It is extremely important that anxiety be kept to the minimum. The teaching and learning of spelling can be fun—and we none of us need to be reminded that we tend to repeat actions that give us satisfaction and evade or actively resist repeating those that cause unhappiness and loss of prestige and self-confidence.

A formal spelling lesson

As an example of mutual enjoyment of a formal spelling lesson may I describe one approach I have found successful?

Write	here	on a chalkboard
	here	in a column
	here	eight times
	etc.	

Ask the children to read what is written. Then say 'Shut your eyes!' Add t to the second line, thus:

here
there
here
here

and say 'Open. What has altered? Good. Read it.' Choose a child and say 'Please do as I ask. Come here.' When this has been done

'Good. Go over there!' and point. 'Good. What does here mean? There?' It causes some amusement if after you have called another child to 'Come here', you move round the room so that he has to chase you. In turn add prefixes to each word in the same manner until you have completed here, there, where, nowhere, elsewhere, somewhere, anywhere, everywhere. As revision ask the children to shut their eyes and then rub a word off. 'Open. Which word has gone? What does it mean? Who can put it back?' Finally issue duplicated sheets with 'here' written eight times in the original column. Ask questions yourself—or better still, encourage the children to ask questions—to which one of these words is the answer. The children fill in sheets to match. As soon as possible, use these words in a P.E. lesson and perhaps test the spelling again the next day.

Spelling games

Other spelling games that children enjoy and which prove profitable are heads and tails.

Put up one letter   a

Ask 'Who can add a head or a tail?'

                      at

'Good. Who can add another head or tail?' and so on.

Or take a starting point such as

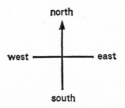

and try to collect more of the same kind. Some children like to call these 'families'. Encourage the writing of them by aligning letters to emphasise the common letters or clusters, e.g.

        east   east

                  not

      beast   beast

This sort of activity fits in well with the study of rhymes and the writing of verse. At first it is probably enough to collect true rhymes

east
least

but later encourage partial rhymes such as

east   or   ea
easter   east
redbreast   tea
                          break

linking visual and auditory 'rhymes', so that awareness is increased for cues for spelling. At this point, small card tiles with letters on them are extremely useful and remove the need to write in order to try out letter sequences and combinations. Although historically writing preceded reading, reading will often precede writing/spelling in children as the latter demands a double code—the physical ability to make a mark on paper turning sound to meaning—whereas reading does not simultaneously demand additional muscular co-ordination of writing. On the other hand, it is certain that the act of writing does help children in learning to read! The two are inescapably interwoven, and nervous impulses are fed back to the brain from the hand. It is therefore extremely important that errors should be kept to the minimum. Mistakes lay down electrical circuits as powerfully as accuracies. For this reason, it is unwise to put inaccurate spellings on a chalkboard and then request children to correct them. You may teach the faulty spellings in this way, and thus increase the children's chances of failure.

Another point to keep in mind is the slower rate of development in males. The calcium is not usually deposited in a man's skeleton until the age of twenty-two or thereabouts—but is normally complete in a woman's about the age of eighteen. Hence the girl of four is the physical equivalent of a boy of five. The muscle and bone distribution in their bodies is also progressively different—girls can turn cart wheels earlier than boys—but boys have less weight in their pelvic girdles and better muscles in chests and arms for climbing, and usually excel in these pursuits. We should therefore expect slower motor co-ordination in boys than girls—but as well as this being considered, we need to realise that neatness is the adult concept, and only slowly accepted by children as a reasonable aim. In order to win approval, however, they may early have the ability to produce exquisitely neat work for one adult, while transferring nothing of this level of presentation to other areas of their lives!

Summary The teaching of spelling must include visual, auditory and kinaesthetic perceptual cues. Emphasis should be on stressing similarities rather than differences; letter groups rather than individual letters. Presentation usually should call attention to spelling cues.

brown		(*a*) brown down owning
down	not	or
owning		(*b*) brown
		down
		owning

Teaching techniques and spelling activities

1 *Develop accurate speech* If you are used to saying 'panny' for penny or 'ford a bolit' for 'fired a bullet' it is entirely consistent and reasonable to spell incorrectly.

2 *Listening games and activities* are essential to the development of the listening ear. They should be enjoyable to ensure attention and the wish to play them again. Play 'I spy' with letter sounds, not names. Make charts of things with same initial letters—especially b and d. All matching and sorting games with whole words, and later initial, middle and endings are useful. Breaking words like 'carrot' into car and rot and the converse—making words out of smaller ones 'not ice' attract some children. Some children attend better if they make a physical response such as standing, waving, jumping, clapping, etc., to a spoken sound or a flashcard.

'Which word sounds the same as
    or   looks the same as
    or   looks and sounds the same as
cat? "Dog, sheep, bat, not?" '

3 *One cue at a time* but link visual and auditory where possible—prefixes and suffices:

big	break	east	saw	sag
boy	broom	feast	sawn	prig
ball	branch	beast	awning	dig

later centre letter sequences

moon	meat	fire
soon	bead	girl
balloon	real	shirt

and arrange to accentuate similarities.

Which of the foregoing have visual cues?
Which of the foregoing have auditory cues?
Which of the foregoing have both?
NEVER homonyms

4 *Colour* is not helpful when it breaks the outline, e.g. shop and even whole words in colour may confuse as certain colours stand out more than others.

Colour is both personal and emotive and we must be on our guard against making false associations or interfering in individual colours or the significance they carry. The same argument is valid when criticising the use of colour in number indicators:

●	❂ ❂	○ ○ ○	⊘ ⊘ ⊘ ⊘
1	2	3	4

5 *Relevance of words taught*, i.e. motivation. Link spelling lessons to the needs of the children. We learn best at the moment we *want* to know. Sometimes contrasts are easily learned at the same time—perhaps 'rough' could be contrasted with both 'smooth' and 'gentle'?

6 *Establish alphabet order* as stage three in the use of picture dictionaries. Picture dictionaries seem to be more effective to children in this order:

Stage 1   Individual interest—one child's collection
Stage 2   Relationship—sheet of toys, food, family
Stage 3   Alphabetically—sheet of b.

Cards can then be used, arranged in alphabetical order, possibly in open shoe boxes or similar containers.

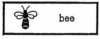

Stage 1   word and picture
Stage 2   word one side, picture on reverse

Stage 3   word, plus other uses of the same letter sequence

bee—same as tree

see

seed

feed

with a relationship list on the obverse

bee   hive

honey

sting

egg

grub

7 *Children's own dictionary* is only useful when the children have a secure grasp of the alphabet (and trick digraphs such as ph on a p page!) and have the power to look quickly down a page and *recognise* the word they seek. Every teacher has been asked for the spelling of a word already written on the board or in the child's book —which proves the problem still facing the questioner—that of finding it to copy. Address books are useful for word 'storage'.

Commercial dictionaries are on sale in many forms—but most are of little use until quite a high degree of spelling competence has been achieved.

8 *Graded lists* depend for their usefulness on the compiler's understanding of the early stages of learning to read and spell. There are four types of spelling grouping:

(*a*) Similar auditory and visual elements

power   shower   tower

(*b*) Similar visual, dissimilar auditory elements

stove   glove   prove

(*c*) Dissimilar visual, similar auditory elements, i.e. homonyms

bier   beer

their   there

bear   bare

(*d*) (1) silent letters (2) trick digraphs or (3) illogical

gnat, knight, smile, island, two, ele*ph*ant, *ch*urch, *th*umb, *wh*om, once, *ch*oir 'v' *ch*at

There are several types of relationship grouping:

(*a*) common elements and context

    e.g. double letters n*ee*dle   bu*tt*on   co*tt*on

                          tr*ee*   be*e*ch   s*ee*d

(*b*) context

    milk, water, tea, coffee, lemonade
    father, mother, son, daughter, baby

(*c*) element of difficulty

    (i) silent letters

knee	comb	mate
kneel	crumb	hive
knock	thumb	mile
knob	climb	some

    (ii) illogical pronunciation although, rough, cough, though, bough, lough

    (iii) plurals

mouse	mice	day	days
house	houses	lady	ladies

Word counts have produced helpful lists (see pp. 86–7) of words which figure most and least often in children's speech. It may tempt some people to 'drill them in' but this is short-sighted and could simply de-motivate.

9 *Diagnosis of difficulty* is essential before attempting to teach the children. Some common causes of mistakes are:

motor—i.e. mis-writing
visual—i.e. mis-seeing
faulty hearing   } leading to inaccurate representation
faulty pronunciation } of sounds
confusion of meaning—common with homonyms
inability to analyse sequence of sound or even ignorance of how
    to represent it

Where possible, link meaning with spelling:

               hear with ear,   sea with beach

but on another occasion: beech with tree or I, with mine, their.

Direct word observation through context and word family; tongue twisters; jokes and puns; rhymes (initial-tail—mid-word); relationships; trick spellings and catches (mispronunciation helps here—g—nat, com—b, k—night, etc., and helps to reduce anxiety). Praise phonetic spelling even if wrong—it shows a logical reasoning

approach. N.B. 'ellifunt' may exactly match the voiced sounds.
Exaggerate eleph*ant* and make a collection of f sounds spelled ph.

10 *Important teaching points* are recognised by the increased
interest and success of the children learning to spell—and the confident attack on complicated and expressive words. Praise for an
interesting word should be generous—and the correct spelling perhaps only offered if a fair copy is wanted. It is better to correct too
seldom than too soon.

Numerous short periods of teaching are more effective than fewer
long ones.

Words in our active vocabularies are easier to learn than those in
our passive vocabularies.

Rhythmic repetition is especially appealing to infants and juniors.

11 *Spelling games* such as Lexicon, Scrabble, codes, anagrams,
crosswords, word building are valuable. So are:

> The Parson's cat (i.e. listing adjectives in alphabetical order);
> Pack your suitcase (i.e. listing contents similarly);
> Alphabet Matching;
> Sorting and setting words;
> Heads and tails;
> Beheading and adding new letters;
> Filling in blanks—add all or ill;
>   dr— k—ed sh—ing f—ing v—age h—s
> Pairing words for rhyme; visual similarity, meaning; opposites;
> relationships of meaning, spelling, sound, rhythm, etc.; identical
> letters (saw, was) etc.
> With advertisements, old magazines or reading books—ring all
> letter d in red, syllable at in green, s in yellow, b in black and so on.

Make collections of words with double letters or all made from
one word like PHEASANT; words which contain another word (mat is
found in matter, formation, mattress), words which have a long e
sound (piece, seed, reads, these, teeth) or i sound (aisle, sight, height,
my, mine, choir).

There are many more to be found in work books but the best ones
are those invented by the children themselves.

Seven points for success

Success is heavily dependent on:

1 the development of right attitudes towards spelling, viz. interest,

self-confidence, spelling 'conscience', i.e. courtesy to your reader; intention to remember, positive 'attack'

2 motivation—the idea of the usefulness of clarity of communication

3 teaching geared to individual needs

4 definite and efficient methods

5 emphasising progress and 'rewarding' it with unforced pleasure at the child's success. N.B. reinforcement of mutual pride in achievement.

6 revision, especially at the moment when a word is moving from passive to active vocabulary, because of relevance

7 systematic and immediate remedial work.

Test yourself!

I How quickly can you find out what is unusual about this paragraph? It looks so ordinary that you would think nothing is wrong with it. In fact, nothing is; but it is distinctly odd. Why? Who knows? Go to work and try your skill.

II *Crack this code*

Decode the following message:
GUVF VF N SNVEYL FVZCYR PBQR IREL RNFL GB QRPBQR GURFR PBQRF NER NYJNLF RNFL

III *Test of genius*

Read the following sentence slowly:
'Finished files are the result of years of scientific study combined with the experience of years.'

Now count the number of F's in the sentence. How many?

I The most common letter in the English language is E, but there is not a single E in the paragraph. II 'This is a fairly simple code, very easy to decode. These codes are always easy.' III A person of average intelligence finds 3. A person of above average intelligence finds 4. If you got five you can turn up your nose at anybody. If you caught all six, you're probably a genius and you ought not to waste your time taking tests like this!

Spelling jingles

There follows a collection of spelling jokes, visual and auditory, but the truths contained within them highlight the problems of learning to spell in English:

Hints on Pronunciation for Foreigners

I take it you already know
Of tough and bough and cough and dough?
Others may stumble but not you,
On hiccough, thorough, laugh and through?
Well done! And now you wish, perhaps,
To learn of less familiar traps?

Beware of heard, a dreadful word
That looks like beard and sounds like bird,
And dead: It's said like bed, not bead—
For goodness sake don't call it 'deed'!
Watch out for meat and great and threat
(They rhyme with suite and straight and debt).

A moth is not a moth in mother
Nor both in bother, broth in brother,
And here is not a match for there
Nor dear and fear for bear and pear,
And then there's does and rose and lose—
Just look them up—and goose and choose,
And cork and work and card and ward,
And font and front and word and sword,
And do and go and thwart and cart—
Come, come, I've hardly made a start!
A dreadful language? Man alive.
I'd mastered it when I was five!

only initials of writer known: T.S.W.

Anglo-Saxon Noises

Sir,—I have been pondering for some time on the vagaries
of the English language and its illogical pronunciation. For
instance, there are six ways of pronouncing 'ough', involving
at least fifteen words. On listing them, I was tempted to write
a 'Shakespearean sonnet' incorporating them as an aid to those
foreigners who are doubtless struggling with them:

Weary with toil, I reach my home at Slough;
All the day long I have not ceased to cough:
I hear the birds that twitter on the bough,

The horses stamp while drinking at the trough.
My health is poor because my work is rough.
I like the job and mean to keep it, though
My mother says the pay is not enough
For one who spends his life in kneading dough.
She thinks I ought to walk behind the plough
And go to join my Auntie up in Brough,
Where rain and hail and all the winds that sough
Will brace my body and will make me tough.
But I'll not leave my home and native borough,
But stay and work. My motto shall be 'Thorough'.

However, I then found there was an odd man out, without
a rhyme, so I appended this:

But now I come to reading this right through,
I must conclude I may be starting flough.

Salisbury   Mrs Dora H. Robertson

Will you please explain to me Why in 'debt' you should use
    silent b?
I cannot gebt the hang of it yebt in fact I'm completely at sea!
You say that the ocean is blue is a warship then manned by
    a crue?
Do you give a receipt to the man in the streipt? It puscles me
    all the day thrue.
If a man dies you say he is dead but a book, not the colour,
    is read.
Still I think that's enough of this terrible stough goodbuy, Sir—
    it's past tyme for bead.

Hough Nough!

The spelling of English is a pitfall for most of us at some time
or another; here are some oddities for your amusement.

Sob Story

Today, away from me you fly,
Though, yesterday, to me you flew,
So now I am disposed to cry,
Though heretofore I never crew.

Not Hard to Swallow

I wonder what would help my cough;
A cup of coughey should.
At least it wouldn't bump me ough,
And it might do me gould.

Companion Peace

A jug of wine beneath the bough
And milk from yon contented cough
And you beside me makes me glow
Deliciously, from head to tow.

The Point is Moot

If you say, 'Boot',
Then why not foot?
And on your feet,
You should wear beet.

An eccentric chap named Turner recently began signing his name Phtholognyrrh. Pressed for an explanation, he justified his bizarre orthography as follows:

phth, as in phthisic, is pronounced	T
olo, as in colonel, is pronounced	UR
gn, as in gnat, is pronounced	N
yrrh, as in myrrh, is pronounced	ER

11　Summary

'More haste—less speed'.
'Look before you leap'.

It is odd that there is no accepted training for the most important profession in the world—parenthood. It is frightening that although the state since 1973 had offered free full-time education for eleven years there are still adult illiterates in our country. At first sight there may appear to be little connection between these two statements—the connection in my mind is that there is still far too wide a gap between the parents who, perhaps unconsciously, set out to educate their children by 'bringing-them-up' and the schools that consciously set out to educate children by training teachers for three or four years in order to do so.

The Plowden Report, 1967, Children and their Primary Schools:

At the heart of the educational process lies the child. No advances in policy, no acquisitions of new equipment have their desired effect unless they are in harmony with the nature of the child, unless they are fundamentally acceptable to him. We know a little about what happens to the child who is deprived of the stimuli of pictures, books and spoken words; we know much less about what happens to a child who is exposed to stimuli which are perceptually, intellectually or emotionally inappropriate to his age, his state of development, or the sort of individual he is. We are still far from knowing how best to identify in an individual child the first flicker of a new intellectual or emotional awareness, the first readiness to embrace new sets of concepts or to enter into new relations.

Knowledge of the manner in which children develop, therefore, is of prime importance, both in avoiding educationally harmful practices and in introducing effective ones. In the last 50 years much work has been done on the physical, emotional and intellectual growth of children. There is a vast array of facts, and a number of general principles have been established. This chapter is confined to those facts which have greatest educational significance and those principles which have a direct bearing on educational practice and planning.

Among the relevant facts are the early growth of the brain, compared with most of the rest of the body; the earlier development of girls compared with boys; the enormously wide variability in physical and intellectual maturity among children of the same age, particularly at adolescence, and the tendency nowadays for children to mature physically earlier than they used to. Among the principles are present-day concepts about critical or sensitive periods, about developmental 'sequence' (that is, events which are fixed in their order but varying in the age at which the sequence begins); about the poorer resilience of boys than girls under adverse conditions; and above all, about the complex and continuous interaction between the developing organism and its environment. Under this last rather cumbersome phrase lies the coffin of the old nature-versus-nurture controversy. A better understanding of genetics and human biology has ended the general argument, and provided a clearer picture of what is implied when we talk of changes in measured intelligence during a child's development.

The nature–nurture controversy

The heredity versus environment controversy is age-old but what makes us what we are or prevents us being what we are not? Can we choose? To what extent are we dependent on the chemical balance of our bodies? Is it true that we 'behave' because we 'feel'? If we cannot control our feelings, can we control our behaviour? Is it true when we say 'I couldn't help it'? Who bears responsibility for the behaviour of children: the parent, the teacher, the child? What do children bring with them to school at the age of five? Why? What are the characteristics of a good parent? What are the characteristics of a good teacher?

It is the writer's view that the better the home and school understands each other, the better the chances are that the children will mature satisfactorily, and in their turn become 'good' parents. As so many teachers nowadays are also parents this should not be too difficult to achieve—but, in fact, there is still a deplorable amount of suspicion and distrust between some homes and schools, and we shall all have to make a real effort if the situation is to improve.

There is no doubt that there is a close correlation between behaviour problems and the inability to read. It is therefore in the interests of all three—parent, teacher and child—that learning to read should be an experience that is as pleasurable as possible and that results in confident and efficient grasp of language skills; the ability to converse, read and write, with the maximum degree of communication. (This is obviously not suggesting the converse, that children who *can* read will be exempt from behaviour problems!) However, we must try to ensure that the words we ask children to read are of interest to them and within their experience. Children must enjoy words, understand the uses of writing words and reading books, have experiences they are eager to share and have opportunities to practise talking and listening, writing and reading, and recording in many ways. One child returned home after his first day at school and told his mother 'I'm not going to school again. I can't read and I can't write and they won't let me talk, so I think it's a waste of time.' How right he was, and luckily, few such schools exist today! We now realise that children who are seen and not heard are being prevented not only from developing speech and the understanding of language—but being deprived of the opportunity of developing intelligence also. Nor can the responsibility for teaching children to read be laid entirely on the schools. As long as the legal age for starting school is the term after the fifth birthday the most important period for developing language is past, and it is widely accepted that time lost in the pre-school years cannot be fully made up subsequently. It is therefore all the more vital that parents become aware of how much they can do for their children before handing them over to teachers for much of the day.

Dr Joyce Morris reported on her survey in Kent to the International Reading Association on 25 May 1964, and described the best teachers thus:

These teachers in the top 'A' grade made a great effort to improve their classroom environment, showed a keen interest in their pupils' progress, enjoyed reading themselves and were interested in research in reading and education generally. They believed that all children, unless officially classified as educationally sub-normal, could achieve adequate reading standards by the end of the primary course, and, if some failed to do so, it was the result of unsatisfactory school conditions. In other words, they felt that the children's initial handicaps, either in themselves or their home circumstances, could be overcome with sympathetic understanding and determination on the part of the teachers. These 'A' teachers had an extensive and deep knowledge of reading methods and materials. In practice, their methods were appropriate and imaginative for all pupils, whilst they used the books provided in the best possible way. For instance, they carefully graded class library books and checked whether they had been read by orally questioning their pupils and by making their written commentaries. Additionally, in allocating other books, they made sure that they were appropriate in difficulty and maturity of content for the recipient. Finally their discipline was excellent in that it was apparently effortless, and their charges were not only well-behaved, but they worked industriously and happily.

The writer is not quite so optimistic—feeling that with the present size of class it is not possible to give the degree of individual help that some children need if they are to overcome the influence of their environment. Nevertheless some teachers perform perhaps near miracles in the service of the children they teach. Full individual records permit the best possible use of time available; coloured sellotape on the spine of books can guide the children to those within their capacity and a wide knowledge of different methods and activities allows selection to meet individual interests and needs. When this is supported by parents who give the all-important love and interest to their children that is the essential for healthy growth and development then children are likely to learn to read—economically, efficiently and pleasurably. These fortunate children are then set free to cross the barriers of time and space. They have access to writers long dead or far removed geographically, they can share ideas with people of different interests and cultures, and they can set their own thoughts—either in speech or writing— before their contemporaries or maybe their descendants. From a more utilitarian standpoint, they are enabled to find information, pursue information and study the 'subjects' into which mankind has divided the seamless robe of knowledge. From a purely mercenary point of view they will be better able to earn a living and exist comfortably in a civilisation that depends greatly on numeracy and literacy. Small wonder that adults have always set such store on learning to read and write!

There probably never was a period in history when the anxiety of the adult to train the young to conform to existing patterns of life and society did not sometimes overlook the nature of children and their ways of learning. As young children are so anxious to please—almost fatally so—let alone being so helpless and dependent in their early years of life—it was easy to mould them into any shape. Those that resisted would either be appealed to (or threatened?) through love for parent/teacher, duty to either/both, or where considered 'necessary', compelled by force and punishment. The content of the work considered suitable was chosen less to fit in with children's interests than to ensure that they conformed to a certain ideal. This was frequently to become adult as soon as possible and to reach a common standard. It is only comparatively recently that the aim has altered into that of studying each child individually and then trying to help him to make the most of his gifts, compensate for his shortcomings, learn to know his powers and to be considerate of his fellow creatures.

Making good use of childhood

It is not chance that man has such a long period of immaturity, he has most to learn and the highest capacity to do so. Nor have we the excuse of ignorance. There is, of course, much that we do not know about human development, the turning of the human brain into a human mind and the way in which to learn to live together and not to destroy our planet. On the other hand, we pay lip-service to the needs of young children yet continue to build an environment for the majority which cuts drastically across the needs of children and virtually ensures that many will not reach their potential. No one who has looked at the way in which children behave when allowed to play freely can possibly believe that physical well-being and emotional stability have no influence on powers of learning. Intellectual needs are as great, and these can only be met by interested adults. Children do not choose their environment; they play with what lies before them, and for some children there is tragically little to play with. The desirable response of children to a rich environment (rich in the sense of playspace and material to handle, NOT money) is exploration, experiment and speech. A sympathetic adult to share pleasure; to ask and answer questions; to support and encourage; stimulate and restrain; appreciate and criticise makes it possible for children to move from egocentricity (self-awareness) towards social maturity; from ignorance towards understanding of the environment; from helplessness to independence yet successful human intercourse. We need to be able to give *and* receive.

This development from a helpless baby to a mature adult is not a painless process, either for the children or the adults who nurture them. Children do not *like* being 'brought up'! They test to the full the maturity of the adult—and we in our turn have to display wellnigh superhuman self-control and powers of judgment. When do we respond to the baby or young child as he *is*, when do we seek the older child or adult he is *to be*? How long do we wait for him to discover for himself, how soon should we interpret or teach? How do we discover the way in which his mind works or try to explain the way we think? Few people now think of children as blank sheets on which to write or empty suitcases to be filled with facts; we are cautious about teaching them facts or skills before they understand their importance; we try to ensure that effort is not diverted either to acquire rewards or to avoid punishment.

The acquisition of intelligence and language

We can be unnerved by the knowledge that the early years are so vital in the acquisition of intelligence. About 50 per cent occurs during the first four years, a further 30 per cent before eight and only 20 per cent between eight and eighteen, but developmental stages are infinitely more important than chronological ages and individual differences more important than theoretical standards. Those of us who have spent many years teaching young children have proved over and over again that the 'more haste—less speed' approach is infinitely more constructive than the traditional 'forcing the pace' to a common goal. Where children are involved and understanding, they will spare themselves no effort—willingly undertaking real drudgery in order to achieve their aims. Spectacular progress will be made in a few weeks, more than is made in months (or even years) when their interest and understanding is not ensured. As a result of so-called progressive methods, i.e. those founded on natural learning processes, a significant rise in academic standards has been achieved and work once only thought suitable to secondary schools is being undertaken in junior and infant schools. On the other hand, we now leave until later many of the more mechanical processes knowing that a few weeks is sufficient when the required readiness is present.

Observation, assessment and records

It is this assessment and stimulation of readiness that is the major responsibility of the teacher of young children. Careful observation and cumulative records are an essential. It is obviously impossible to carry all aspects of physical, intellectual, social and emotional development of thirty or more children in one's mind. It is also obviously very helpful if parents will brief the school on the pre-school development of their children and continue to keep the school informed of significant events in their children's development. Attitudes and emotional responses are of the utmost importance—

particularly as they affect language development so closely. We do not want children to develop into unthinking talkers, learning by rote like a parrot or budgerigar; nor should they imitate unthinkingly like apes and monkeys. It is all too easy to create an environment in which children strive to speak and behave as they believe adults desire—children who seek to buy approval and love and do not feel they are of value in themselves.

Handbook of Suggestions for Teachers: 'Perhaps what a child needs most is to be allowed to be himself and to find that this self is liked and appreciated.'

It is for the adults who care for him to be careful to distinguish between subjective and objective judgments; the trivial and the important; the immediate and what will wait, so that in our handling of the children we keep them secure in our love even while we may not and should not accept their behaviour. As Eileen Molony wrote, 'There is only one definition of a good teacher—he or she makes it possible for children to learn what they need to know.' Parents are, of course, teachers too and all adults who serve children must remember that the feelings of children make it possible or impossible for them to learn—even what they need AND wish to know.

Tests, marks and examinations

There are far fewer tests, marks and examinations in schools nowadays—undoubtedly a good thing. Many people erroneously believe examinations to be as objective as a tape measure, whereas, however hard we may try to construct an objective test, so much personal assessment is part of them. Percentages and competitive lists can have severely, even permanently, damaging effects on people's belief in themselves. Just as we cannot expect everyone to be identical in physical make-up—as worker bees are when hatched—so we cannot expect everyone to have identical powers. If powers are not identical then standards cannot be either, and the modern practice of encouraging children to compete against their own performance is the only acceptable one, especially in earlier years of life. Many adults now recognise that their only superiority to children is that of experience and, that unless they have made good use of such experience, children may well be further advanced than the adults they meet. Every teacher has had at least one pupil considerably cleverer than himself/herself—though it may not always please adults to recognise this fact.

Competition and punishment

For this reason, and the fact that change is breathtakingly rapid at this period of history, it may be impossible for any adult to know, for certain, what it is worthwhile for children to learn. We are educating them for so unpredictable a future that adaptability and self-confidence are probably what matter most. My own working life as a teacher has covered over three decades and in this short time the large measure of agreement as to *what* children needed to know and hence *now* they should be taught, on which I was trained, has given place to a certain amount of confusion and disagreement. I suppose adults have always fallen into the two main divisions—those who believe children want to learn, and those who believe they must be compelled to do so. If you believe the latter, punishment is logical and public glory or humiliation an effective weapon. Some schools even sat children in an order which called attention to performance. It would seem likely that a pupil in third place might strive for the excitement of moving to second or first—but can anyone seriously believe there is an equal incentive to moving from fortieth to thirty-seventh? The sad truth is that if *someone* is first, then someone else is last, and that *most* of us soon fail to believe in our worthwhileness if those around us continually call it in doubt. There is no truer statement than 'Give a dog a bad name and hang him'. Luckily its converse is equally true and children rise to the expectations of those they love and trust, so that many schools today seek to give each child a belief in himself and his powers to succeed. He should slowly acquire a knowledge of his talents and problems, so that the most can be made of his gifts, his difficulties recognised and as many as possible removed, and an ability to live with the rest developed.

Teaching reading in the junior school

As a result of our growing understanding of how children may best learn to read and our knowledge of the problems that an unsatisfactory environment can breed in children, many children will be unable to master the mechanics of reading in the infant school. Teachers in junior schools will therefore carry much of the responsibility for helping children to read and will therefore need to possess the techniques required. It is hoped therefore that colleges of education will give comprehensive courses in the teaching of reading; that schools will see that parents are informed as to how they can help, and that infant and junior teachers will exchange ideas and thus raise the level of individual teaching and remove unnecessary disappointment from their pupils. After the mechanical skill of reading has been acquired there is need for continuing motivation to ensure enough practice to lead to effortless fluency—to be followed by more advanced skills such as scanning; skimming; content recognition and recall; reading aloud for audience appreciation; silent reading at many levels of speed and thoroughness, and the special skills demanded for reading poetry, verse and prose drama, comedy, tragedy and the like.

The modern primary school and its ethos

Many parents are suspicious at the freedom given in primary schools today—confusing it with licence. The ability to choose wisely takes time and practice to learn. Play is the means of independence and survival; the way of learning and the desire to learn. Therefore we build our learning on the play instinct, because this is far more economical and efficient than forced labour. Obedience, on occasion, is of course essential, but passive obedience is very dangerous indeed: this is what allows dictators to establish themselves. We must think for ourselves and take responsibility for what we do. Therefore for much of the day the children choose their work and how long they spend on it. Only in this way do they learn to concentrate, persevere, complete a difficult job, turn failure into success and learn to plan time wisely. On other occasions the teacher will call a group, a whole class or even several classes together for a shared experience or direct teaching. This may be a traditional type 'lesson' or an occasion for joint effort or a time when music is shared, a story told or read, a period for learning to listen or appreciate the efforts of other people. Throughout the day and week the teacher will see that each child receives a balanced education, covering all areas of the curriculum, but not necessarily at the same time or pace as his peers.

Throughout the day we try to give children the chance of working with older and younger ones. This is very important. Before they come to school the children have passed through their major learning period. Never again, in the course of their whole lives, will they change so much in a comparable span. We hope that their parents will have enjoyed being with their children; talked and listened to them; shared books and toys and games with them; taken them on walks and visits; helped them to enjoy rhymes and songs;

to welcome visitors and be pleasant guests in other people's homes; to be kind to smaller children and creatures; to be unafraid of new people and experiences. Obviously the children have had *different* experiences, even being the oldest, youngest or middle child in a family makes an enormous difference to life. So, when they reach school they *need* different things. Some children need to repeat an experience; explore a new material; play at a younger stage, without feeling babyish or self-conscious. Others need to nerve themselves to attempt what they believe too demanding; to watch older or more skilled children; to have a rest or stand and stare.

So the children are encouraged to move around the school, sensibly and courteously. They learn that teachers have different skills and interests. They enjoy studying displays in various parts of the school; look at models and pictures made by their friends; talk with the caretaker, cook or visitors to schools, and in other ways have their interest aroused and their standards of performance raised. They learn where to find the help or the information they need, and the usefulness and economy of tool subjects such as reading, writing and mathematical skills.

Whatever job they do in life we believe we shall need people who are able to think for themselves; to work independently at times and closely and happily with other people on other occasions; who can communicate with other people by words and actions—so that misunderstandings do not arise—who can accept that other people do not think as they do but that this makes life more interesting; who recognise that knowledge is increasing so fast that many 'facts' are no longer true almost as fast as they are learned; in fact, people who have a healthy knowledge of and respect for themselves and are thus able to live at peace with other human beings and give them respect, support and friendship.

The more we know about other people and their ways the easier it is to understand them. The literature of the world records man's interest in himself; his discoveries; his thoughts and beliefs; his hopes and fears; his love and his cruelty; his optimism and his pessimism. We must obviously do all that we can to give a child the key that unlocks this storehouse and hope that he himself will add to it.

Conclusion

1 *Book list* No book list is included because the writer feels that it would have to be very extensive if it were to direct further reading on the content of this book.

Public libraries, and particularly librarians interested in books for children are always most helpful—and the best source of information for parents.

Students in training have, in addition, access to their college libraries—and professional advice from their tutors.

Practising teachers in infant and junior schools will first be concerned to make the best use of the books and reading materials in their schools, and to supplement this with home-made and commercially prepared apparatus as funds allow. Most schools set aside a yearly sum to spend on books. Some local education authorities provide special loan collections of books. Some teachers have access to teachers' centres, in-service courses and exhibitions of books such as those that can be hired from the National Book League, or the Tann Collection from the Department of Education and Science, available to Her Majesty's Inspectors. Teachers are also usually made welcome in consulting the librarians and libraries in local colleges of education. Some universities provide library access or special libraries for teachers. Special technical advice can be expected from teachers of remedial reading and educational psychologists.

2 *Commercial material* As previously suggested, it is most important that the teacher's manual be studied before the use of any graded reading scheme.

Materials and apparatus need critical assessment. The cost of buying an item must be set against the cost of raw materials and the time involved in making it. Versatile apparatus which is permanently needed is probably worth buying. Some practice material should be expendable and can easily be made on a standard duplicator. Other games or apparatus must be devised for an individual child and may need to be expendable also. It is a mistake to feel that care in the making is not necessary. Guillotined edges; a high standard of lettering; in matching material that really *is* identical; even the prestige of having it made 'for me alone' are all part of setting the scene—and will help children to raise their own levels of work.

As so much teaching nowadays is individual there is a major need for self-corrective apparatus, or supplementary material that can be marked by the child concerned. Not only does this save valuable time —but it engenders a valuable attitude of responsibility and independence in the pupil. Many children like to work in pairs, checking their own and each other's work and this attitude of co-operation is infinitely preferable to the traditional competition, and anxiety to get marks or status symbols such as stars.

Teaching machines may have a place in the classroom but the initial expense and their servicing and maintenance are not inconsiderable problems. Some children are emotionally unable to learn without the constant support of a teacher and the early hopes of being able to replace teachers by machines, language laboratories, etc., have lessened. In specialist conditions, such as remedial teaching—some children seem helped over specific difficulties through the use of a machine in a most encouraging way.

Cassette tape recorders are specially useful in normal classrooms— and very young children handle them with ease and confidence.

3 *Index* It has not been thought necessary to provide an index, but chapter content is referred to under chapter headings. There are plenty of technical books on the teaching of reading to which reference can be made for detailed techniques or extra ideas for classroom activities. Teacher's manuals are also useful for the latter.

4 *Radio and television* Both these media if well prepared for and intelligently followed up have a place in the primary school. For very young children, this is probably less than at first hoped for—the problem being that personal contact with other people is so important for communication. 'Teaching distance' for young children is normally within arm's length—and for some children only within physical contact. A voice from a box—or the face on the screen—is not an efficient substitute for the teacher.

As listening and verbal powers develop, so the radio and television programmes become more valuable but they depend largely on their presentation by the teacher.